Smiling

*Smiling is infectious, you catch it like the flu
When someone smiled at me today I started smiling too.*

*I passed around the corner and someone saw me grin
When he smiled, I realised, I'd passed it on to him.*

*I thought about a smile and realised its worth
A single smile like mine could travel round the earth.*

*So, if you feel a smile again don't leave it undetected
Let's start an epidemic quick and get the world infected.*

Why Bumble Bees?

I adore Bumble Bees, They are so beautiful and extremely useful as important pollinators.

But my love of Bumble Bees started with a Bumble Bee necklace, given to me on the birth of my eldest son Guy, by my beloved husband. When I asked one of my little grand-daughters what she would like to call me she said "*Bumble like your necklace*".

"I LOVE FOOD" 3

By Clare Macpherson-Grant Russell

Clare Russell is Lady Laird of the romantic
Ballindalloch Castle and retired Lord Lieutenant of Banffshire.

Following on from the success of her cookery book series,
'I Love Food' and 'I Love Food 2', Clare now presents
a third helping of recipes reflecting her love of easy home
cooked food, family and the ravishing Speyside
surroundings she adores. Her motto as ever is:
Simply delicious, simply elegant.

All the Family

To My Darling
'Chief Taster'

Live well,
Laugh often,
Love much.

Introduction

I never thought that I would write another cook book, but I have so many more delicious recipes, tried and tested over the last few years, that I'd like to share with you that I couldn't resist – so, here I go again!

As I was listening to my favourite radio programme, 'Desert Island Discs', I realised what enormous fun it is to hear about other people's lives! So I thought that I would do a 'through the keyhole' introduction, setting out a few landmarks in my life, along with recipes and some photographs throughout the book to match.

I'll start at the beginning, with a little background of my family. Ballindalloch, my home for 70 years, has always been a much-loved family home, where my relations have lived since 1546. It is one of the very few castles to have been lived in by the same family for over 450 years, and I am the 22nd generation of my family to do so – and also the first 'Lady Laird'. I arrived at Ballindalloch in 1950 when my father inherited the castle from his cousin, Sir George Macpherson-Grant, and probably from that moment my life was paved out. It was made clear to me from an early age that it was my duty, as the only child, to carry on the family heritage - and in those days you did as you were told! I had a wonderfully happy childhood at Ballindalloch and, although sometimes a little lonely, I had Cammie, my lovely governess, who

taught me everything I know. She was a 'Wee Free' lady and a daughter of the Manse, so on a Sunday, the Lord's Day, I was allowed only to read the Bible and go for nature walks. I was brought up on Robert the Bruce (think of the spider and 'try, try again') and 'idle hands are lazy hands' and 'money doesn't grow on trees'. I think that Cammie might be smiling down on me now, as I had the great honour a few years ago of receiving an honorary degree from the University of Aberdeen for my work in Banffshire, something of which I am extremely proud.

At 18 years of age I went to the bright lights of London, where I was offered a job by Constance Spry, who had been creating a sensation with her flower-arranging business. I remember ringing my father in great excitement to tell him the news; there was a long silence, followed by a horrified "Young ladies don't take jobs; they get married and have children!". I accepted the position, and so began my long-lasting love affair with flowers and gardens. I then started my own flower business, making the most wonderful friends in the old days of Covent Garden Market; it was just like My Fair Lady! The East-enders were all wonderful, and I am afraid I must have stood out like a sore thumb amidst them, but they all became the greatest of friends, and I was always known as the 'bonnie wee lassie from Scotland'. I would not have missed those few years for anything.

Then I did the best thing in my life I met and married Oliver, an Englishman! I did make it quite clear that the arrangement had to be 'love me, love my castle, love Scotland' but, most important of all, 'love my dogs'! It was a big undertaking and sacrifice for Oliver, who had to give up his banking career in London.

We spent the following forty years entertaining corporate parties at Ballindalloch, and we also opened our doors to the public. Our corporate guests enriched our lives and we met many amazing people, from television personalities such as Monty Don and the Hairy Bikers, to Hollywood stars like Billy Connolly and Kurt Russell. The earnings from the corporate parties helped us to modernise every room in the Castle, as well as fifty estate houses, our hotel, and our shop and tearoom.

My love of gardening really arose from my flower-arranging days in London, and when I arrived at Ballindalloch I had great aspirations that the garden there would soon look like Covent Garden; what I hadn't realised was that south Banffshire is one of the most difficult growing areas in the country! I shall always remember meeting the Head of the National Trust Gardens just after I had returned north, and his asking me if I was a gardener. I replied "Yes, I am, but I am a very amateur one". Where did I garden? "South Banffshire". I can see his face now, as he replied "Good God, you will have to be keen to garden there"! Forty years later, I can tell you that he was totally correct. All I can say is that we try to have 'a garden against all odds'. We love alchemilla and nepeta, in fact anything that grows, and we don't worry about colours - God's Garden, after all, is a myriad of colours. One of our more recent projects was to re-design our walled garden into a beautiful rose garden to celebrate the 450th anniversary of the Castle; it has been much admired, and we are delighted to have been featured in the Good Gardens Guide and in several books.

The Banffshire Coast

Looking after the Ballindalloch gardens, the corporate parties, and my dogs has been only part of my daily duties. In November 2002 I was given the great honour by Her Majesty the Queen to become Lord Lieutenant of Banffshire (the Queen's personal representative in the county) and it is a role of which I am extremely proud. It is a great honour and privilege to serve Her Majesty and Banffshire in this way, and I very much hope that I do our wonderful county justice. I am the 11th Lord Lieutenant of Banffshire and, to satisfy my feminist side, the first Lady Lord Lieutenant in Banffshire and the North-east. Lord Lieutenants retire at the ripe old age of 75 years, so I will have served for seventeen years at the end of my term of office. It always amuses me that, in this age of sex equality, a peer's wife is known as a 'lady', whereas a peeress's husband stays a 'Mr', and a lady Lord Lieutenant is still a Lord Lieutenant - with the result that nobody knows what to call me! 'Lady Lord Lieutenant', 'Lady Laird', very often 'Lady Clare', sometimes 'Lady Lieutenant'; indeed, I had a wonderful old housekeeper who wrote a lovely letter congratulating me on my appointment, and ended it with "I never knew you were in the Army"!

The duties of a Lord Lieutenant are probably unknown to most people; my predecessor used to say "A Lord Lieutenant is like a bidet – everyone knows what it is but nobody knows what it is for – but it adds distinction to the room!" My job is, first of all, a very pleasant one. I have the joy of meeting so many different special people from different parts of the county. I have the pleasure, on behalf of Her Majesty, of giving out 100th birthday cards, diamond or platinum wedding cards, honours, and the Queen's awards for voluntary service in the community. I am involved in citizenship ceremonies, the British Legion, the Territorial Army, the cadets and the RNLI. I am involved also in many charities, and in various ways with the Police and Fire Brigade. I help organise invitations to royal garden parties and royal visits, which are enormous fun but which involve considerable work.

Royal Visits & Events

The role of Lord Lieutenant commenced in Scotland in 1794, and the first Lord Lieutenant for Banffshire was the Earl of Fife from Duff House. A Lord Lieutenants' principal role was to rally troops for the king from their particular counties. Luckily, we don't have to do that now, but I still have the honour to be involved with the Army, the RAF and the Royal Navy; indeed, I was privileged to be invited to tour round the new aircraft carrier 'The Prince of Wales', and also the P8 reconnaissance plane which replaces the Nimrod.

The most delightful duties, of course, are when members of the royal family visit Banffshire. In my seventeen years as Lord Lieutenant we have been honoured to have had about 40 visits from members of the Royal family.

One of the most important and memorable occasions of the last two years was the Gordon Highlanders' Victoria Crosses Commemoration Parade and Gathering, when It was my enormous honour and privilege to stand in for their Colonel in Chief, HRH the Duke of Rothesay. Also in the last few years I have laid four stone slabs in memory of the four VC holders who lived in Banffshire, and gave the ultimate sacrifice. What an honour for our small county.

Last year Banffshire has surpassed itself with the amazing church services, laying of wreaths, and poppy nets made by the community, to remember those who never came home. Our schoolchildren, too, have been hugely impressive, with their events and researches on the men who were educated at their schools and gave their lives for future generations.

In January last year we organised a visit by HRH The Princess Royal to open the amazing renovations at Banff Academy and the Myrus Stadium. Her Royal Highness was due to arrive by air at Lossiemouth at 10am; the aeroplane arrived and circled 1,000 feet above, but due to the horrendous gale was not allowed to land at Lossiemouth, or any other nearby airport! It was a nightmare, as I had over 1,000 pupils and guests waiting for the royal arrival, so there was no alternative but for me to be a Princess for the day! Generously, Her Royal Highness immediately suggested another date, so we had the pleasure of entertaining her on another day.

The last twelve months have been a real landmark year for me, especially as I was presented with a CVO from Her Majesty the Queen; an incredible honour. Also, this last year Oliver and I celebrated our Golden Wedding, which was very special. I really have been so lucky to have been given a wonderful life.

One of my reasons for writing 'I Love Food 3' is to tell you of our great excitement about the building of our little distillery, that we started in 2014. Oliver and I were sitting in front of the fire one evening discussing a dilapidated steading on the estate. It was clearly visible from the main road and we agreed that it was letting down the look of the estate. We did not want to bulldoze it to the ground, and it was in the wrong place for a retail outlet. In a moment of inspiration, Oliver said "Why don't we build a distillery – whisky is in your DNA!" He was correct, as my great-grandfather Sir George Macpherson-Grant, along with the famous distiller John Smith, had built Cragganmore Distillery in 1869. Unfortunately, my father had to sell his share of the distillery for tax reasons in the 1950s.

The distillery has been a true family collaboration Guy focussed his energy on the business plan and the structure; Edward oversaw the project management and the application for grant funding; I designed the interiors of the Long Gallery and the Family Room; and the whole project was overseen by Oliver. We are incredibly lucky that we have the perfect access and position on the A95 on Speyside, and that we benefit from seven beautiful springs on the hill behind the distillery. The distillery is totally integrated with the estate and sustainable. We grow our own spring barley that is used to make the whisky; our famous Aberdeen Angus cattle eat the draff; the pot ale fertilises our farm field; and the wind farm on the estate offsets the electricity. We are making whisky the old fashioned way.

"I LOVE FOOD"

138 ravishing recipes from the
Lady Laird of Ballindalloch Castle

CLARE MACPHERSON-GRANT RUSSELL

Clare Macpherson-Grant Russell's follow up
to her remarkably successful BEST SELLER

"I LOVE FOOD"
2

I hope this letter finds you well. Thank you so much for your help when I telephoned about the two cookery books, it was much appreciated.

All the books arrived promptly and I am absolutely capped with them. I gave a copy of "I love food 2" to my mother and she is thrilled, having used the first book extensively. I too cannot wait to put the receipts to use on the dinner party circuit.

Please pass my thanks and congratulations to Mrs. Russell for the simply divine books. So user friendly and well thought-out.

I'd like to end this glimpse of the 'landmarks' in my life with some stories about my books. I wrote the first little ones because I had so many recipes, concocted and tried over the years of entertaining our corporate parties. So many people enjoyed them that I decided to write my first hard back book 'I Love Food', which has been an amazing success and is still selling after fifteen years and over fifteen re-prints. 'I Love Food 2' followed eight years later. 'Third Helpings' wasn't really on the cards, but I received so many lovely e-mails asking for a further taste that I couldn't resist putting pen to paper again. In this book I have again included a selection of my favourite poems and sayings, along with photographs of some of my landmark events of the last two years. My beloved dogs have a section, of course, and they thoroughly approved of their special recipes, most of which were baked by my, 'doggie masterchef', my grand-daughter.

You might think, if you watch television, that everyone aspires to cooking like a celebrity chef, but in reality few of us have the time. I don't presume at all to be a 'master chef' – just a home cook who loves traditional food. I have two recipe categories; 'posh food' and 'comfort food', and in my books I try to show how even easy recipes can be made 'simply elegant'.

'I Love Food' and 'I Love Food 2' have been enormous fun, and because of them I have made such lovely friends and acquaintances. The two books have found their way to most of the British Royal Family and some of the European Royal families, as well as the White House. Several years ago, just before Christmas, I had a call from an American lady saying that she was going to spend the holiday with very special friends who had everything, but she thought they wouldn't have my book. Could I sign it for them? The first book was to be signed 'to Barbara', and the second was for Laura! What a privilege to have my little books in the White House! One other very special story concerns the occasion when I was given the privilege of presenting Her Majesty The Queen with her 80th birthday present on behalf of the Scottish Lord Lieutenants. While waiting for Her Majesty to arrive, her Private Secretary turned to me and asked if I wrote cook books. "Yes", I replied. He then went on to tell me that he had just come from the kitchen where, while he was talking to the head chef, his eyes had alighted on a very scruffy book filled with post-it notes. He asked the chef if he used 'I Love Food', to which chef replied "Constantly, look at the post-it notes; in fact, we are having one of her puddings today"!

Guy, our eldest son and family at
Ballindalloch Castle

Pitchroy
Lodge

After many years at Ballindalloch Castle, we have now 'downsized' to Pitchroy Lodge, a delightful house looking over the River Spey to Ben Rinnes, and our eldest son, Guy, and his family have moved into the Castle; this is wonderful as I was the last in my family and there were no brothers or sisters or close cousins to inherit.

Pitchroy has an interesting history. It was rented for many years by Captain W.E. Johns of 'Biggles' fame, and many of his books were written here. Also, Her Majesty the late Queen Mother fished here with her nephew, the late Lord Elphinstone.

I do hope you have enjoyed my introduction. I have been so lucky to have been given such a wonderful and varied life, and I feel privileged at my age still to have a very full one, with many challenges and great happiness. I only hope that I have given back a little to this world as well. I would like to end with one of my favourite poems, 'Success' by Bessie Anderson Stanley; I find her words so inspiring.

*She has achieved success who has lived well
laughed often and loved much;
Who has gained the respect of intelligent men
and the love of little children;
Who has filled her niche and accomplished her task;
Who has left the world better than she found it;
Who has looked for the best in others and given
the best she had;*

Clare Macpherson-Grant Russell.

19

Menu

Cool Canapés

Canapés are very fashionable at the moment as it saves making a starter and gives you more time with your friends.

Smoked Salmon on Blinis with Crème fraîche & Mock Caviar

Croustade with Poached Quail's Eggs with a Spot of Hollandaise

Croustade with Prawns in Seafood Sauce

Pâté on mini Porridge Oatcakes

Cheese Sables with Chopped Walnuts or Sprinkled with Streaky Bacon

Croustades with Scrambled Eggs, Sprinkled with Crispy Bacon

Parma Ham with Goats Cheese on Blinis

Super Soups

As Molière wrote: I live on a good soup, NOT on fine words

Mushroom & Stilton

(Serves 4-6)

INGREDIENTS

½ lb (225g) fresh mushrooms plus
 ¼ lb (100g) for slicing
1 oz (25g) butter
1 oz (25g) flour
1 pt (600ml) good strong stock
 (preferably home-made; stock cubes are
 usually inferior in taste and texture)
½ pt (300ml) double cream
2 tablespoons crumbled Stilton
seasoning

METHOD

Make sauce with the butter, flour and
stock. Liquidise mushrooms and add
to sauce. Simmer for 10 minutes. Add
cream and sliced mushrooms, season
and heat gently. Add crumbled Stilton at
the last minute.

Celeriac & Apple

(Serves 4-6)

INGREDIENTS

1 tablespoon olive oil
1 large celeriac, peeled and
 cut into ½ inch chunks
knob of butter
4 small potatoes sliced
1 green apple peeled, cored and
 cut into ½ inch chunks
1 onion finely chopped
1¼ pts (700ml) vegetable or chicken stock
¼ pt (150ml) apple juice
seasoning
seeds and cream for decoration

METHOD

Melt butter and oil in large pan, add
onion and stir till soft. Add diced celeriac
and potatoes to pan and cook for about
5 minutes till celeriac is slightly coloured.
Add diced apple with stock. Cover pan
and cook for 20 minutes till vegetables
are soft. Remove pan lid and cook for a
further 5-10 minutes. Add some apple
juice to taste. Liquidise with stick blender,
season. Sprinkle with a swirl of cream and
some toasted seeds.

Spinach & Pea

(Serves 4)

INGREDIENTS

1 onion (finely chopped)
1 garlic clove
2 tablespoon (40ml) olive oil
½ teaspoon (2.5mls) ground cumin
1 lb (450g) spinach leaves
8 oz (225g) fresh or frozen peas
2 tablespoons chopped mint
1½ pts (900ml) chicken stock
freshly grated nutmeg
seasoning
Parmesan or chopped fried bacon

METHOD

Heat oil in pan and add finely chopped onion, garlic and cumin. Fry gently till transparent. Wash and dry spinach leaves. Cut out hard stalks and shred roughly. Add to pan with peas mint and stock. Bring slowly to boil, cover and simmer gently for about 15 minutes. Place in liquidiser and process till very smooth. Return to pan and heat gently till boiling point. Add seasoning. Sprinkle with chopped bacon or grated parmesan.

Scotch Broth with Diced Chicken

(Serves 4-6)

INGREDIENTS

For the Stock:
chicken bones or "cheat" with a stock cube
1 onion
2 carrots
2 sticks celery
parsley
2¾ pts (1.5l) water

To make the Stock:
Place bones in large pan with ingredients, simmer for 1½-2hours.

2 chicken breasts cooked and chopped finely
1 onion peeled and chopped
2 carrots peeled and diced
2 medium potatoes peeled and diced
2 tablespoons olive oil
1 tablespoon finely chopped parsley

METHOD

Sauté vegetables in large pan till soft 10-15 minutes, add stock, simmer for 20 minutes, add chicken. Cook for another 5-10 minutes. Season, sprinkle with parsley.

Beetroot, Parsnip & Apple

(Serves 4)

INGREDIENTS

1 tablespoon olive oil
1 large onion chopped
1 apple peeled and chopped
1 parsnip peeled and chopped
1 small potato peeled and chopped
4 large beetroot scrubbed and chopped
2 pt (1.2l) vegetable stock
4 tablespoons crème fraîche
horseradish to taste
seasoning
bunch of parsley

METHOD

Heat oil in large saucepan and add onion. Sauté for a few minutes until soft. Add apple, parsnip, potato and beetroot. Stir. Pour over vegetable stock, cover and simmer for 25-30 minutes. Place in liquidiser or use a hand stick blender, until smooth. Place crème fraîche in bowl and add horseradish. Add black pepper to taste. Ladle soup into bowls, top with teaspoon of crème fraîche and a sprinkling of parsley.

Leek & Stilton

(Serves 4-6)

INGREDIENTS

3 oz (75g) butter
5 oz (150g) stilton cheese
1 lb (450g) leeks
3 tablespoons flour
2 pts (1.2l) chicken stock
¼ pt (150ml) single cream

METHOD

Slice and wash leeks. Fry gently in butter till soft. Crumble in cheese and stir till melted. Add flour and cook for 3 minutes. Gradually add stock and seasoning. Simmer until leeks are cooked, liquidise and pour into clean pan. Reheat and add cream. Serve.

Beetroot, Parsnip and Apple Soup

Tomato & Rosemary

(Serves 6)

INGREDIENTS

8 oz (225g) chopped onions
1 teaspoon chopped fresh rosemary
3 x 400g tins of tomatoes
  (or equivalent weight in fresh tomatoes)
2 teaspoons tomato purée
1 oz (25g) sugar
1½ pt (900ml) chicken stock
1 level tablespoon cornflour
½ pt (300ml) single cream
seasoning
chopped parsley for garnish

METHOD

Place the chopped onions, rosemary, tomatoes, tomato purée, sugar and stock in a large pan. Remove a little of the stock to cream the cornflour. Add the blended cornflour to the pan cover it and simmer all the ingredients for approximately 20 minutes. Remove from the heat and liquidise. Adjust the seasoning. Reheat and stir in the cream just before serving. Serve very hot with a garnish of chopped parsley.

Watercress & Parmesan

(Serves 4-6)

INGREDIENTS

1 oz (25g) butter
1 onion finely chopped
2 bunches of watercress,
  washed and chopped
1½ pts (900ml) vegetable stock
¼ pt (150ml) single cream
1 oz (25g) plain flour
seasoning
grated fresh parmesan

METHOD

Melt butter in large saucepan, add chopped onion, cook till soft. Add watercress, cover and sweat for 10 minutes. Stir in flour and cook for a minute. Add stock stirring well so the flour has no lumps. Bring to boil and simmer for 5 minutes. Cool slightly. Blend till smooth in Magimix or stick blender. Stir in half the cream. Season. Re-heat soup through, pour into bowls to serve. Garnish with a swirl of remaining cream and sprinkle over with grated parmesan cheese.

Cullen Skink with Lobster Pieces & Prawns

(Serves 4-6)

INGREDIENTS

1 oz (25g) margarine
4 undyed smoked haddock fillets about
  8 oz (225g) each
½ onion, chopped
4 potatoes (preferably Kerr's Pink or
  other floury variety) peeled and diced
2 teaspoons cornflour
3 pt (1.75l) milk
4 tablespoons single cream
seasoning
1 packet prawns
lobster pieces (optional)

Raising the Cullen flag

METHOD

Melt the margarine in a large saucepan. Skin and break haddock in large pieces. Add haddock and onion to pan and cook gently for 2 minutes. Par-boil potatoes until almost tender, then drain. Mix cornflour and 1 tablespoon cold milk. Add remaining milk and potatoes to saucepan and bring to the boil. Stir in the cornflour and simmer for 2 minutes. Add prawns and lobster pieces. Just before serving, stir in cream and season.

Sensational Starters

Avocado Mousse Topped with
  Prawns & Lobster Seafood Sauce 32

Eggs Benedict with Parma Ham,
  Sliced Avocado & Poached Eggs
  Served on a toasted Baguel with
  Hollandaise Sauce   34

Baked Quails Eggs with Asparagus
  in a Cream & Parmesan Sauce 35

Avocado, Pink Grapefruit & Parma
  Ham Salad in a French Dressing 35

Hot Smoked Salmon Kedgeree
  with Turmeric & Poached Egg
  or Quails Eggs   36

Penne Pasta with Lobster & Prawns
  in a Cream & Parmesan Sauce 37

Pan Roasted King Scallops Served
  on a Pool of Creamed Spinach
  Sprinkled with Chopped
  Streaky Bacon   38

Fan of sliced Avocado & Mango
  with Prawns in a Seafood Sauce 40

Pear & Prawn Delight   42

Fresh, Ripe Comice Pears with
  Parma Ham & Goats Cheese 42

Twice Baked Soufflés with a Cream,
  Prawn & Lobster Sauce   44

Pea Panna Cotta Decorated with
  Swirls of Smoked Salmon & a
  Blob of Hellmans Mayonnaise 46

Rough Chicken Liver Pâté
  with Prunes & Pistachios   48

Smooth Chicken Liver Pâté   48

Smoked Salmon &
  Quail's Egg Tartlets   50

Spinach Mousse with Parma
  Ham Swirls & Mini Balls
  of Melon Served with
  Home-Made Mayonnaise   52

Kenny's Salmon Terrine   54

Baked Field Mushrooms with
  Cream Cheese & Stilton   55

Smoked Salmon Sandcastles
  Filled with Fresh Crab & Served
  with an Avocado Sauce   56

Spicy Mushrooms with
  Garlic Bread   58

Cucumber Mousse with Avocado
  in a French Dressing   60

Smoked Haddock Mousselines
  with a Prawn &
  Hollandaise Sauce   62

Avocado Mousse Topped with Prawns & Lobster Seafood Sauce

(Serves 6)

INGREDIENTS

2 avocados
3 leaves of gelatine
½ pt (300ml) of mayonnaise
squeeze of lemon juice
small white wine glass of dry white wine
  or chicken stock
dash of Worcestershire sauce
seasoning
jar of seafood sauce (M&S)

For the Base of Glass:

1½ cucumbers (skinned, sliced,
  with core removed and chopped finely

For the Prawn/Lobster Sauce:

1 bag (180g) prawns
A few cooked lobster pieces (if possible)
jar of mock caviar

METHOD

Place 3 gelatine leaves in bowl and cover with water to soften. Pour wine or stock into pan and warm over gentle heat. Remove gelatine from water, squeeze to remove excess water and dissolve in wine. Leave to cool. Then fold in mayonnaise. Peel, halve and stone 2 Avocados. Liquidise. Add to mixture, season and add dash of Worcestershire sauce. Pour over finely chopped cucumber in martini glass. Leave to set for 3 hours.

Just before serving, mix jar of M&S Seafood Sauce with Prawns and Lobster pieces, pour over Avocado Mousse. Decorate with mock caviar.

To Die For – My favourite of all starters

Eggs Benedict with Parma Ham, sliced Avocado & Poached Egg Served on a Toasted Baguel with Hollandaise Sauce

(Serves 4)

INGREDIENTS

4 large eggs
4 large slices of fresh parma ham
4 Baguels (toasted)
4 ripe avocados
  (stoned, skinned and halved)
hollandaise sauce
parsley for decoration
knob of butter

For the Hollandaise Sauce:
4 egg yolks
1 tablespoon water
2 tablespoons lemon juice
6 oz (150g) melted butter
seasoning

METHOD

Poach eggs lightly, split and toast baguel. Butter. Place Parma Ham on top of baguel followed by sliced Avocado followed by poached eggs. Then drizzle with Hollandaise and decorate with parsley.

For the Hollandaise Sauce:
Whisk egg yolks, water and lemon juice in bowl over hot water. Pour in hot melted butter and whisk till thick. Season.

P.S. If it curdles add an ice cube and whisk like mad!

Baked Quails Eggs with Asparagus in a Cream & Parmesan Sauce

(Serves 4)

INGREDIENTS

12 quails eggs
12 asparagus
  (tips only - make rest into soup)
4 tablespoons grated parmesan cheese
1 pt (600ml) double cream

METHOD

Heat oven to 325°F/160°C/Gas 3. Crack
3 eggs into each of 4 ear dishes. Pour
cream carefully around eggs. Blanch
asparagus in pan of boiling water. Cool
a little and cut tips off asparagus. Add to
eggs, sprinkle with parmesan and bake
for about 10 minutes until set.

Avocado, Pink Grapefruit & Parma Ham Salad in a French Dressing

(Serves 4)

INGREDIENTS

4 pink grapefruit
4 oz (100g) parma ham
6 oz (150g) rocket salad
2 avocado pears
French dressing
  (buy from M&S if you are feeling lazy)
1 tablespoon poppy seeds (optional)
1 lemon

METHOD

Peel, stone and halve the avocados. Slice
lengthwise and sprinkle with lemon juice.
Peel grapefruits and cut into segments.
Cut Parma ham into 1" strips. Arrange
rocket leaves like spokes of a wheel,
then place segments of grapefruit and
avocado alternately on top. Curl the strips
of Parma ham into cone and place in the
middle. Sprinkle with French dressing and
poppy seeds.

Hot Smoked Salmon Kedgeree with Turmeric & Poached Egg or Quails Eggs

(Serves 4)

INGREDIENTS

6 oz (350g) brown basmati rice

6 oz (350g) hot smoked salmon, skinned and flaked

1 tablespoon vegetable oil

1 large onion, finely chopped

12 green cardamom pods, split open

1 teaspoon turmeric

4" (10cm) cinnamon stick

3 bay leaves

1 pt (600ml) chicken stock

3 tablespoons chopped fresh parsley

1 teaspoon white wine vinegar

4 large eggs or 12 quails eggs

METHOD

Cover rice with water and leave to soak for 10 minutes. Meanwhile, heat oil in large saucepan. Add onion and cook gently for 5 minutes until opaque. Add turmeric and bay leaves. Cook for minute. Drain rice, and add to the saucepan stirring well. Add stock and a little salt and pepper, bring to boil and stir. Cover with a lid and cook gently for about 30 minutes. Uncover rice, remove bay leaves. Gently fold in hot smoked salmon, cover again and cook slowly on low heat for about 5 minutes until fish is heated through Stir in parsley and season to taste. Keep warm. Meanwhile, poach eggs in boiling water with a teaspoon of vinegar. Take out gently with slotted spoon and top each plate of kedgeree with a poached egg or quails eggs.

Penne Pasta with Lobster & Prawns in a Cream & Parmesan Sauce

Turmeric is suddenly everywhere and is supposed to be a cure for everything from heart disease, cancer, alzheimer's, depression and arthritis! So, I thought I must add some to one of my recipes. I believe it can be added to most things such as scrambled eggs, roasted vegetables, cauliflower, rice, chicken or vegetable soup.

(Serves 4)

INGREDIENTS
6 oz (150g) penne pasta
4 oz (100g) smoked salmon
1 packet prawns
Lobster pieces
1 oz (25g) butter
4 oz (100g) fresh parmesan cheese
½ pt (300ml) double cream

METHOD
Cook pasta in pan of boiling water according to instructions on packet. Cut smoked salmon in thin strips. Melt butter in pan, stir in double cream, smoked salmon, prawns and lobster pieces. Heat gently for 5 minutes. Drain pasta and toss it in the cream sauce. Sprinkle with Parmesan cheese and cook for another 5 minutes.

Pan Roasted King Scallops Served on a Pool of Creamed Spinach Sprinkled with Chopped Streaky Bacon

(Serves 4)

INGREDIENTS

12 king scallops
clarified butter for pan frying
streaky bacon (grilled until crispy)
2 fl oz (50ml) double cream (optional)
seasoning
2 packets creamed spinach

METHOD

For the Spinach:
Heat spinach gently in pan. If mixture is too thick to blend easily, add a few drops of cream. Season to taste with salt and pepper. Re-heat gently for serving.

For the Scallop:
Pan-fry scallops in butter for 1-2 minutes each side, depending on size, and serve on a pool of creamed spinach. Sprinkle with crispy streaky bacon and serve immediately.

I adore scallops, but they can be tricky

Fan of sliced Avocados & Mangos with Prawns in a Seafood Sauce

(Serves 4)

INGREDIENTS
2 avocados
2 mangos
1 packet Prawns
seafood sauce (M&S)
parsley for decoration

METHOD
Halve, peel and de-stone avocados. Peel mango and slice. Sprinkle sliced avocados with lemon juice (to stop going brown). Place sliced avocados and mangos in fan shape. Mix prawns with seafood sauce and place in centre of fan. Sprinkle with parsley.

Looks so pretty on a glass or white plate

Pear & Prawn Delight

(Serves 6)

INGREDIENTS

3 large pears
4 tablespoons seafood sauce (M&S)
6 oz (150g) prawns
seasoning
mock caviar to decorate

METHOD

Peel pears and halve lengthwise. Scoop out core. Sprinkle with lemon juice. Mix prawns with seafood sauce. Place in middle of pears and top with mock caviar. Serve with brown bread and butter.

Simple is delicious

Fresh, Ripe Comice Pears with Parma Ham & Goats Cheese

(Serves 4)

INGREDIENTS

4 large comice pears
1 round goats cheese (cut into 4)
1 bag of mixed leaves
8 slices parma ham
French dressing

METHOD

Peel pears carefully keeping stalk on. Slice off bottom of pear and place in middle of each plate. Place mixed leaves all round, tear Parma Ham into six pieces and place on leaves. Dot Goats cheese around. Dribble with French dressing.

Twice Baked Cheese Soufflés with a Cream, Prawn & Lobster Sauce

(Serves 6)

INGREDIENTS

½ pt (300ml) milk
2 oz (50g) butter
2 oz (50g) flour
pinch of dried mustard
6 oz (150g) cheddar cheese
2 tablespoons parmesan cheese
4 eggs plus one extra egg white
½ pt (300ml) double cream
nutmeg
½ lb (225g) prawns
lobster pieces
seasoning

METHOD

Melt butter, flour, mustard and milk slowly together whisking like mad till it comes to boil. Add ¾ of the cheese and seasoning. Separate egg and add egg yolks to sauce. Whisk all whites and fold into cheese mixture. Spoon into buttered cocotte dishes filling almost to the top. Stand in bain-marie (a baking tin half-filled with hot water) and bake for 15 minutes at 350°F/180°C/Gas 4. Cool and leave in cocottes. Twenty minutes before dinner, run a knife round soufflés to loosen and turn onto 6 ear dishes. Pour cream over soufflés, add prawns and lobster pieces sprinkle all over with cheese. Bake at 350°F/180°C/Gas 4 for 10 minutes. Serve immediately.

Simply delicious

Pea Panna Cotta Decorated with Swirls of Smoked Salmon & a Blob of Hellmans Mayonnaise

(Serves 4)

INGREDIENTS

1 packet smoked salmon
3½ fl oz (100ml) single cream
7 fl oz (200ml) double cream
3½ oz (85g) frozen peas (de-frosted)
1 small packet prawns
3 sheets of gelatine
1 cucumber (sliced and peeled)
2 tablespoons chopped chives
1 bag rocket leaves

METHOD

Prepare 4 ramekins by brushing them lightly with oil and adding a disc of baking parchment to the base. Heat both creams in pan (do not boil). Add cream to liquidiser with peas, chives and a few rocket leaves and seasoning. Mix, sieve and place back in pan. Soak gelatine leaves in bowl of cold water for 5 minutes. Once softened squeeze out excess water and add to warm cream mixture in pan. Mix well to dissolve. Place 1 prawn in middle of ramekin and then pour mixture over. Repeat with others. When cool place in fridge for at least 8 hours to set. To serve dip base of ramekins in hot water and turn out onto plate. Decorate with sliced cucumber all round panna cotta and with swirls of torn smoked salmon.

Rough Chicken Liver Pâté with Prunes & Pistachios

(Serves 6)

INGREDIENTS

8 oz (225g) chicken livers
  (take off white fat if any)
4 rashers streaky bacon
2 finely chopped onions
8 prunes (stoned)
5 oz (150g butter)
6 finely sliced mushrooms
seasoning
1 oz (25g) pistachio nuts
  (shelled and chopped finely)

METHOD

Fry onions and sliced mushrooms in pan until onions are translucent. Place in bowl. Add chicken livers and fry until cooked – slightly pink in the middle. Add stoned prunes. Mash all roughly with fork, fold in finely chopped pistachio nuts and place in pâté dish. Leave in fridge to set for at least 2 hours. Then cover with melted butter. Serve with hot bread.

Smooth Chicken Liver Pâté

(Serves 4-6)

INGREDIENTS

4 oz (100g) butter
1 finely chopped onion
8 oz (225g) chicken livers
8 oz (225g) cream cheese
seasoning
1 tablespoon Ballindalloch whisky
4 rashers grilled bacon

METHOD

Melt butter and fry onion till transparent. Add chicken livers (cut away any veins) and fry till just pink in the middle. Place in liquidiser with cream cheese and process. Add seasoning. Place in pâté dish and fold in finely chopped grilled bacon. Cool. If wished, melt some butter and pour over top of pâté. Chill and serve with melba toast or oatcakes.

Rough

Smooth

Delicious and different

Smoked Salmon & Quail's Egg Tartlets

(Serves 4)

INGREDIENTS

4 savoury tartlet cases
   (make or buy)
8 quail's eggs
4 oz (100g) sliced smoked salmon

For the Hollandaise:

4 egg yolks
1 tablespoon water
2 tablespoons lemon juice
6 oz (150g) melted butter
A little dill for decoration
seasoning

METHOD

Place tartlets in oven to warm. Meanwhile, make Hollandaise: whisk egg yolks, water and lemon juice in bowl over hot water. Pour in melted butter in steady stream and whisk until thick. Season. Keep warm. Poach quail's eggs in hot water with a little vinegar for about 1 to 1½ minutes. When cooked, but still soft, take out with slotted spoon and place on kitchen paper until dry. Place smoked salmon in tartlets with halved eggs in middle, and pour Hollandaise over the top. Sprinkle with dill. Serve immediately.

Love this

Spinach Mousse with Parma Ham Swirls & Mini Balls of Melon Served with Home-Made Mayonnaise

(Serves 6)

INGREDIENTS

A little soft butter
½ lb (225g) spinach leaves
2 large eggs
1 cup double cream
seasoning
grated nutmeg
6-8 slices parma ham
1 melon (in small rounds)
mayonnaise or crème fraîche

METHOD

Butter base of each dariole mould or ramekin and line with disc of waxed paper. Blanch spinach in a little boiling water for 1-2 minutes. Drain and run under cold water. Squeeze in dish towel till completely dry. Purée eggs and spinach in liquidiser till very smooth. Pour into bowl, add cream and mix, season and add a sprinkling of grated nutmeg. Pour into moulds. Cover each with circle of foil and place in deep baking dish. Surround with hot water. Bake for 20-25 minutes at 325°F/170°C/Gas 3 till firm to touch. Cool, take knife round edge and turn on to plate. Decorate with cucumber and small melon balls.

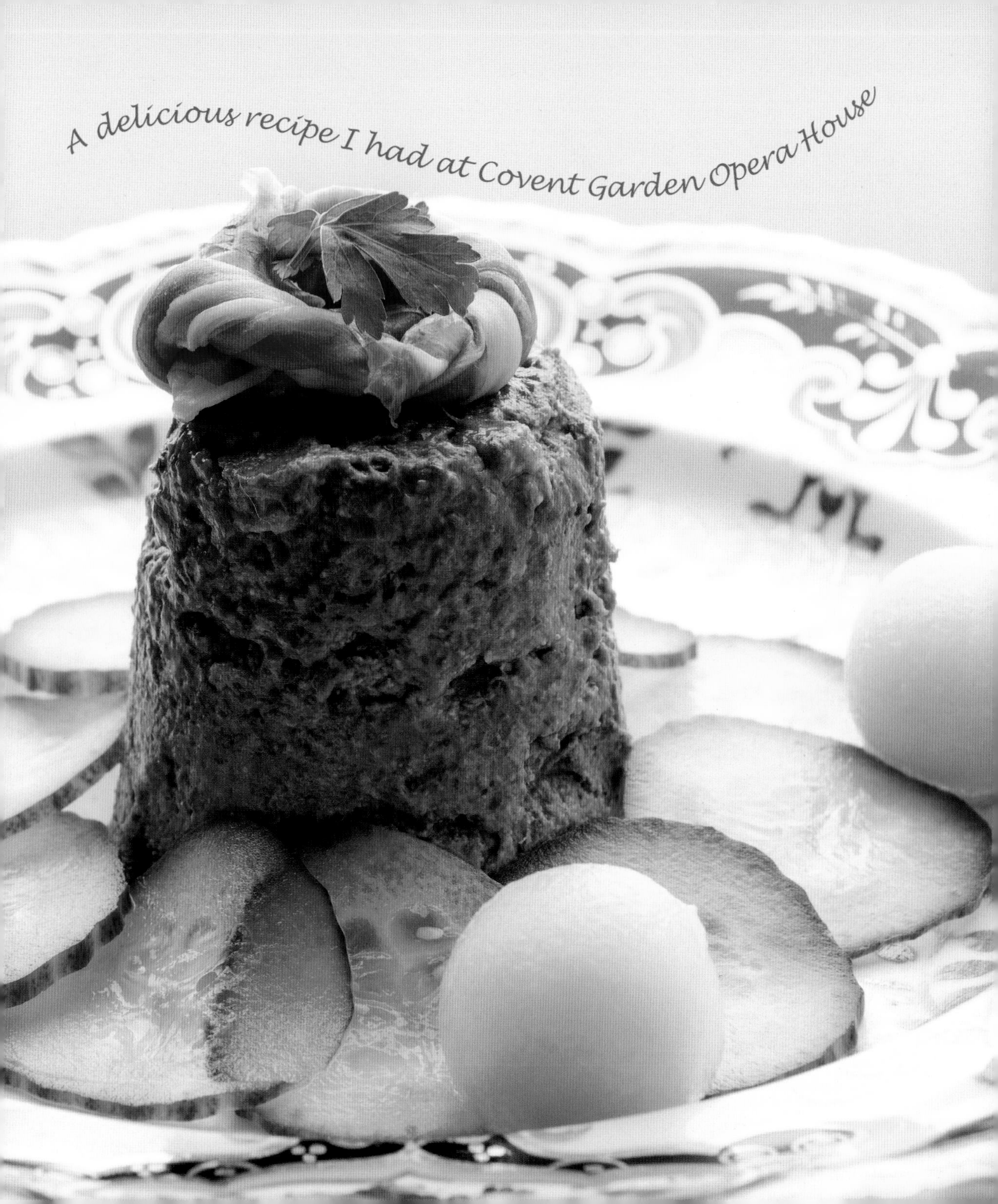

A delicious recipe I had at Covent Garden Opera House

Kenny's Salmon Terrine

(Serves 10)

INGREDIENTS

1-¼ lbs (500g) smoked salmon
   (preferably long sliced)
1-¼ lbs (500g) cooked salmon fillet
3 hot smoked salmon cutlets
3 tablespoons fish stock
8 gelatine leaves (1 packet Dr Oetker
   leaf gelatine) softened in cold water
3½ fl oz (100ml) mayonnaise
3 oz (75g) softened butter
½ pt (300ml) cream
2½ fl oz (75ml)
Juice of 1 lemon
1 tablespoon French mustard
splash of Tabasco
seasoning

METHOD

Line a terrine dish (8cm x 30cm x 6cm) or similar sized loaf tin with smoked salmon, leaving an overhang to wrap over the top of the mousse. Roughly chop trimmings and excess smoked salmon which will later be added to the salmon mousse. Heat fish stock and add the drained, softened leaf gelatine. Place the cooked salmon in a food processor and blend to a smooth purée adding the mustard seasoning, gelatine, mayonnaise, butter and then drizzle in the cream. Quickly pulse in the salmon trimmings along with the lemon juice and sherry. Pour half the mix into the terrine then layer the hot smoked salmon along the middle. Pour the remainder of the mousse on top and fold over the overhanging smoked salmon. Refrigerate for several hours before slicing.

*I could eat this
every day of the year*

Baked Field Mushrooms with Cream Cheese & Stilton

(Serves 8)

INGREDIENTS

8 large field mushrooms with
  deep centre for filling
8 oz (225g) cream cheese
8 oz (225g) crumbled stilton cheese
3 slices white bread
8 slices streaky bacon
  (chopped and fried)

For the Tomato Sauce:

2 tablespoons olive oil
1 finely chopped onion
1 x 15 oz (425g) tin of tomatoes
sugar and seasoning to taste
pinch of dried basil or chopped parsley

METHOD

Mix cream cheese with crumbled Stilton.
Stuff centres of mushrooms with mixture.
Cover with breadcrumbs and chopped
streaky bacon. Bake in a hot oven
400°F/200°C/Gas 6 for 10-15 minutes.
Serve with tomato sauce.

For the Tomato Sauce:

Fry finely chopped onion gently in oil. Add
tomatoes and basil or parsley. Simmer
for 10 minutes. Season and add sugar.
Liquidise. Serve warm.

*So easy and can be
prepared well in advance*

Smoked Salmon Sandcastles Filled with Fresh Crab & Served with an Avocado Sauce

(Serves 6)

INGREDIENTS

8 oz (225g) good white crab meat

8 oz (225g) long thin sliced
smoked salmon

3 fl oz (85ml) natural Greek yoghurt

1 cucumber peeled and sliced
(for decoration)

2 tablespoons seafood sauce or
mayonnaise with a spoonful of
tomato sauce

For the Avocado Sauce:

2 avocado (halved, stoned and skinned)

2 tablespoons natural Greek yogurt

dash of Worcestershire sauce

seasoning

METHOD

Check through crab and remove any shell. Add yoghurt, seafood sauce, chopped coriander and lemon juice. Mix well and season to taste. Rinse out small ramekins with cold water and line with smoked salmon, overlapping edges. Fill ramekins with crab meat and cover with overlapping salmon. Cover with foil and place in fridge for several hours. Turn out carefully, serve with Avocado Sauce.

For the Avocado Sauce:

Place avocados in liquidiser with yoghurt and dash of Worcestershire sauce. Season and serve with smoked salmon sandcastles.

Good party dish, looks pretty

Spicy Mushrooms with Garlic Bread

(Serves 4)

INGREDIENTS

½ lb (225g) mushrooms
¼ pt (150ml) double cream
2 tablespoons tomato sauce
1 tablespoon vinegar
1 tablespoon Worcestershire sauce

METHOD

Fry sliced mushrooms in butter. Place in cocotte dishes. Mix rest of ingredients and pour over mushrooms. Bake in hot oven at 400°F/200°C/Gas 6 for 10 minutes. Serve with warm garlic bread.

These are wonderfully tasty and easy to make.
Can be cooked in the morning and
heated later in ten minutes

Cucumber Mousse with Avocado in a French Dressing

(Serves 4-6)

INGREDIENTS

2 avocados (peeled, stoned and chopped)
6 oz (175g) cream cheese
¼ pt (150ml) cream
2 leaves gelatine (soaked in cold water for
   5 minutes, then squeezed out well)
1 medium cucumber + extra for garnish
2 teaspoons lemon juice
seasoning
¼ pt (150ml) chicken stock
   (preferably home-made)

METHOD

Mix cream cheese and cream together until smooth. Dissolve gelatine (as above) and add to chicken stock. Grate medium cucumber and fold into cream cheese mixture. Add lemon juice, chicken stock and disolved gelatine mixture gradually. Season. Mix well and pour into moulds lined with thinly sliced cucumber. Chill till set. Unmould gently and serve with a blob of home-made mayonnaise and avocados in French dressing with cherry tomatoes for decoration.

A really fresh tasting mousse

Smoked Haddock Mousselines with a Prawn & Hollandaise Sauce

(Serves 4)

INGREDIENTS

10 oz (275g) smoked haddock
2 eggs, lightly beaten
½ pt (300ml) double cream
seasoning

For the Hollandaise with Prawns:

4 egg yolks
1 tablespoon water
2 tablespoons lemon juice
6 oz (175g) melted butter
4 oz (100g) large prawns
seasoning

METHOD

Skin and chop fish. Liquidise with salt, pepper and nutmeg. Blend in beaten eggs and put in fridge for a few hours. Place in liquidiser with cream and process. Butter cocotte dishes well and pour mixture into them. Stand in bain-marie (a baking tin half-filled with hot water) and bake at 375°F/190°C/Gas 5 for 30 minutes. Leave to stand for 2-3 minutes. Turn out and serve with prawn hollandaise.

For the Hollandaise with Prawns:

Whisk egg yolks, water and lemon juice in a bowl over hot water. Pour in melted butter and whisk until thick. Add prawns and seasoning to taste.

My favorite starter you must try it

Marvellous Mains

Fish

Herb Crusted Spey Salmon with Lobster Hollandaise

(Serves 4)

INGREDIENTS

4 fillets of salmon or plaice
  (skinned and boned)
2 oz (50g) freshly grated parmesan cheese
3 oz (75g) stale white bread cut into cubes
3 oz (75g) melted butter +
  extra for greasing
1 bunch parsley
dill to taste
seasoning

For the Lobster or Prawn Hollandaise:
4 egg yolks
1 tablespoon water
2 tablespoons lemon juice
6 oz (150g) melted butter
cooked lobster pieces or prawns

METHOD

Line baking tray with foil and brush generously with melted butter. Wipe fish dry with kitchen paper and lay on foil and season. Whizz cubes of bread, parsley and dill in processor till like fine breadcrumbs. Add Parmesan, melted butter and seasoning. Whizz. Spread mixture onto fish, drizzle a little melted butter over. Place in oven at 400°F/200°C/Gas 6 for about 8-10 minutes, till golden brown. Serve with a lobster or prawn Hollandaise.

For the Lobster or Prawn Hollandaise:
Whisk egg yolks, water and lemon juice in bowl over hot water. Pour in melted butter and whisk till thick. Add lobster or prawns and keep warm.

Always a winner

Sole Meunière with Asparagus

(Serves 4)

INGREDIENTS
4 fillets Sole
a little milk
1-2 tablespoons seasoned flour
3-4 oz (75-100g) butter
seasoning
juice of 1 lemon and 1 extra lemon for decoration
chopped parsley for decoration
1 bundle asparagus

METHOD
Skin Sole. Lay fish in milk and then in seasoned flour. Fry half butter in frying pan and place fish in it. Sprinkle with salt and cook until flesh is golden. Turn Sole carefully and fry till golden. Place in oven-proof dish and cover. Place rest of butter in pan, heat quickly till golden brown. Add lemon juice and chopped parsley. Season, then pour over Sole. Decorate with slices of lemon and serve with cooked asparagus.

A lovely simple recipe for supper

FISHING PARTIES ONLY

Photographs by Andrea de Pree.

Sea Bass on a Bed of Creamed Spinach Served with Mint Hollandaise

(Serves 4)

INGREDIENTS

4 fillets of sea bass
  (skin on scaled and boned)
10 slices of fried streaky bacon
1 lemon
bunch of mint

For the Spinach Purée:
2 packets of cream of spinach

For Mint Hollandaise:
4 egg yolks
1 tablespoon water
2 tablespoons lemon juice
1 tablespoon finely chopped mint
6 oz (150g) melted butter
seasoning

METHOD

Score sea bass skin and place onto non-stick baking sheet flesh side down. Grill for about 5 minutes until flesh starts to flake. Meanwhile, heat frozen spinach in pan. Season. If too thick add a little cream. Warm gently before serving. To serve, place a pool of spinach purée on plate, top with sea bass, sprinkle with chopped streaky bacon, and serve with Mint Hollandaise.

For the Mint Hollandaise:
Whisk egg yolks, water and lemon juice in bowl over hot water. Pour in slowly melted butter and whisk until thick. Season and add chopped mint.

P.S. If it curdles, add an ice cube and whisk like mad!

Always popular

Ballindalloch Salmon Pie with Crunchy Cheese Topping

(Serves 4)

INGREDIENTS

2 salmon fillets (skinned and boned)
2 oz (50g) prawns
2 hard-boiled eggs

For the Sauce:

2 oz (50g) butter
2 oz (50g) plain flour
seasoning and dry mustard
½ pt (300ml) milk

For the Topping:

4 oz (100g) melted butter
6 oz (150g) white breadcrumbs
2 oz (50g) grated cheese

METHOD

Place salmon fillets in oven-proof dish with a little milk. Cover with foil. Bake at 350°F/180°C/Gas 4 for 15 minutes. Melt butter in pan, add flour and cook for one minute stirring continuously. Gradually add milk whisking like mad till boiling point. Add flaked salmon, prawns and hard-boiled eggs. Place mixture into oven-proof dish. Stir breadcrumbs into melted butter and spread over top, sprinkle with grated cheese. Bake at 350°F/180°C/Gas 4 for about 15 minutes.

Salmon en Croûte with a Cucumber & Prawn Hollandaise Sauce

(Serves 6)

INGREDIENTS

20 oz (550g) fresh salmon fillet
   (skinned and boned)
2 oz (50g) butter
1 egg yolk
seasoning
½ pt (300ml) milk
½ pt (300ml) cream
1 packet (1 lb/450g) puff pastry
   (bought puff pastry is excellent and
   a tremendous time saver)
8 oz (200g) sliced mushrooms

For the Hollandaise Sauce:

4 egg yolks
1 tablespoon water
2 tablespoons lemon juice
6 oz (175g) melted butter
seasoning
1 cucumber
   (skinned, cored and chopped)
1 packet prawns

METHOD

Whizz 10 oz (280g) salmon in Magimix with butter, egg yolk and seasoning. Add cream. Roll out pastry into large oblong. Place salmon mixture on top of the pastry in a much smaller oblong (to allow room for folding up). Top mixture with chunks of fresh salmon 10 oz (275g) then sliced mushrooms, salt and pepper and ½ oz butter cut into small pieces. Fold up pastry to form a parcel and if possible shape into a fish. Egg wash and make holes in the top. Bake for 25 minutes in hot oven 425°F/210°C/Gas 7. Serve in slices with a hollandaise sauce.

For the Hollandaise Sauce:

Whisk egg yolks, water and lemon juice in a bowl over hot water. Pour in melted butter and whisk until thick. Season to taste. Add prawns and finely chopped cucumber.

P.S. Hollandaise keeps perfectly for hours in thermos flask. If it curdles, add an ice cube and whisk like mad!

Recipe loved by one and all

Hot Smoked Salmon Quiche

(Serves 4-6)

INGREDIENTS

For the Pastry:

4 oz (100g) butter
6 oz (175g) flour
1 egg beaten and
  1 beaten egg to wash pastry
9" (23cm) loose bottomed flan tin

For the Filling:

1 knob butter
1 onion chopped
4 eggs beaten
½ pt (300ml) double cream
4 oz (100g) hot smoked salmon
4 oz (100g) salmon
2 oz (50g) parmesan cheese
seasoning

METHOD

For the Pastry:

Rub flour and butter till it looks like breadcrumbs. Add beaten egg (it will be sticky) and put in fridge for 10-15 minutes. Roll out pastry and line flan tin. Prick base all over and line with baking paper and baking beans. Bake for 10 minutes at 350°F/180°C/Gas 4. Remove beans and paper. Bake for a further 5 minutes to dry out.

For the Filling:

Melt butter, add chopped onion and cook for 5 minutes. Place in pastry case. Top with flaked hot smoked salmon and fresh salmon. Pour over cream and beaten egg. Sprinkle with the Parmesan cheese. Place on baking tray in oven at 350°F/180°C/ Gas 4 for 25-30 minutes until set and golden.

Excellent with a summer salad

Salmon Fillets Topped with a Herb Crust & Served with a Tomato & Cucumber French Dressing

(Serves 8)

INGREDIENTS
8 salmon fillets
lemon juice & seasoning

For the Herb Topping:
3¼ oz (80g) fresh white breadcrumbs
¾ oz (20g) chopped chives
¾ oz (20g) chopped dill
¾ oz (20g) chopped parsley
3 oz (75g) diced butter
3¼ oz (80g) grated parmesan cheese
3¼ oz (80g) smoked cheddar cheese
good pinch of smoked paprika
good pinch of cayenne pepper

METHOD
Prepare the crust by pulsing the topping ingredients in a food processor gently until it starts to come together. Tip onto work surface and form it into a ball. Roll it out thinly between two sheets of silicone or greaseproof paper and coat the salmon. Bake at 400°F/200°C/Gas 6 for 12-15 minutes depending on the thickness of the Salmon. Serve with a tomato and cucumber French dressing.

Cold Salmon Fillets Topped with Prawns in a Seafood Sauce

(Serves 4)

INGREDIENTS

4 fillets of salmon
1 bunch asparagus

For the Seafood Topping:

1 packet prawns (cooked)
1 jar seafood sauce
crème fraîche to taste

METHOD

Place salmon fillets on baking tray, dot with butter and season and bake in oven at 350°F/180°C/Gas 4 for 10-15 minutes. Cool and top with prawns.

For the Seafood Topping:

Place prawns in large bowl and gradually add seafood sauce. Enough to coat prawns. Place prawns on top of fillet and serve with asparagus.

Looks pretty and so useful

Kenny's Salmon with Soy, Ginger & Chilli with a Mango & Avocado Salsa

(Serves 8)

INGREDIENTS

8 salmon fillets – in an earthenware dish

For the Marinade:
1 tablespoon demerara sugar
1 tablespoon runny honey
2 tablespoons soy sauce
1 teaspoon garlic purée
1 Lime (zest and juice)
1 teaspoon dried coriander
1 teaspoon dried parsley
pinch of salt
1 tablespoon mirren (optional)
¼ teaspoon chilli flakes

For the Avocado and Mango Salsa:
2 tablespoons olive oil
1 red onion
1 red pepper
2 beef tomatoes
2 tablespoons sweet chilli sauce
1 tablespoon runny honey
1 lime (zest and juice)
1 tablespoon cocktail gherkins (chopped)
1 tablespoon cocktail capers
2 ripe avocados
1 packet fresh coriander (chopped)

METHOD

Combine the marinade ingredients in a bowl and pour over the salmon and allow to marinate over night or for several hours ahead of cooking.

For the Avocado and Mango Salsa:
In a bowl, stir together sweet chilli sauce with runny honey and lime. Dice red onion, red pepper and seal off for a minute or two in the olive oil. When cool, add to the bowl with gherkins and capers and coriander. Add diced up avocado and mango to finish the salsa.

Place Salmon fillets onto a foiled baking tray skin side down and pour over the excess marinade. Bake in a hot oven 400°F/200°C/Gas 6 for approximately 10-15 minutes depending on the size of your fish fillets.

Divide salsa between plates.
When cooked lift glazed salmon fillets onto the salsa (leaving behind the skin, which will have stuck to the foil.

Chicken

Chicken Goujons Served with Tomato Sauce

(Serves 4)

INGREDIENTS

5 chicken breasts cut in thin strips
⅓ loaf of white bread
   (made into breadcrumbs)
seasoned flour
1 teaspoon paprika
2 eggs, beaten
1 tablespoon sunflower oil

For the Tomato sauce:

2 tablespoons olive oil
1 finely chopped onion
1 x 15 oz (425g) tin of tomatoes
Sugar to taste
Seasoning
1 pinch of dried basil or chopped parsley

METHOD

Heat oil in frying pan. Dust strips of chicken in flour. Dip into beaten egg and then into breadcrumbs (seasoned and with a pinch of paprika). Fry the goujons gently until crispy and golden. Serve with fried sliced potatoes and Tomato sauce.

For the Tomato sauce:

Fry finely chopped onion in oil. Add tomatoes and basil. Simmer for 10 minutes. Season and add sugar. Liquidise. Serve warm or cold.

The Grandchildren love these.

Chicken Kiev

(Serves 4)

INGREDIENTS

4 boneless chicken breasts (no skin)
4 slices strong cheddar cheese
4 slices good ham
sundried tomatoes (drained well)
3 heaped tablespoons plain flour
2 eggs beaten
4 tablespoons oil
seasoning
7 oz (200g) breadcrumbs
Dijon mustard

METHOD

Drain tomatoes well and liquidise. Make a slit into each chicken breast horizontally and open out like book. Cover with cling film and bash till flat. Remove cling film and place 1 slice of ham and 1 slice of cheese either side. Add a few sundried tomatoes. Fold the chicken breasts over till original shape and secure with cocktail stick. Take three plates. Tip flour onto one and season. Pour the beaten eggs onto another and then add breadcrumbs onto another. Dip each chicken breast into flour, then beaten eggs and then breadcrumbs. Transfer to a large plate. Heat 2 tablespoons of oil in large frying pan over medium heat. Pan fry two at a time for 10-15 minutes until golden brown. Or, you can bake in oven at 200°F/180°C/Gas 6 for 40 minutes.

Love this

Chicken & Mushroom Pie

(Serves 4)

INGREDIENTS

1 lb (450g) chicken cooked
  (3 breasts cooked in oven)
1 onion chopped
½ lb (225g) mushrooms sliced
1 oz (25g) butter
1 oz (25g) plain flour
¼ pt (150ml) milk
¼ pt (150ml) stock

For the Pastry:

4 oz (100g) butter
6 oz (175g) flour
1 egg beaten and
  1 beaten egg to wash pastry

METHOD

Rub flour and butter till it looks like breadcrumbs. Add beaten egg (it will be sticky) put in fridge for 10-15 minutes. Fry onions and sliced mushrooms. Make white sauce with butter, flour, milk and stock. Add chopped chicken, onion and mushrooms.

Roll out pastry. Cut strips to go round rim of pie dish having first egged the pastry. Fill pie dish with chicken mixture. Cover with pastry, wash with egg and cut steam hole in middle of pie. Cook at 350°F/180°C/Gas 4 for 30-45 minutes until golden.

Fricassée of Chicken Topped with Crunchy Bacon

(Serves 4)

INGREDIENTS

6 chicken breasts
  (cooked and chopped in small pieces)
2 oz (50g) plain flour
2 oz (50g) butter
¾ pt (250ml) milk
4 rashers bacon (fried and chopped)
½ lb (225g) mushrooms fried in butter

METHOD

Melt butter, add flour and milk and whisk madly till thick. Add fried mushrooms and chopped chicken. Pour into ovenproof dish and sprinkle top with fried and chopped bacon. Place in oven at 350°F/180°C/Gas 4 for 15 minutes.

Another recipe from the Old Ballindalloch Castle Cook Books

Creamed Chicken with Avocado

(Serves 4)

INGREDIENTS

1 lb (500g) cold cooked chicken
 cut into small pieces
2 oz (50g) butter
2 oz (50g) plain flour
¼ pt (150ml) chicken stock
¼ pt (150ml) single cream
1 tablespoon dry sherry
squeeze of lemon juice
2 ripe avocados
1 oz (25g) grated cheese
seasoning

METHOD

Melt butter in pan, add flour and cook for one minute stirring. Gradually add chicken stock whisking like mad till boiling point. Add chicken pieces, sherry, seasoning and cream. Skin, stone and halve avocados. Slice thinly and cover bottom of oven-proof dish. Sprinkle with lemon juice. Spoon chicken mixture over top and sprinkle with grated cheese. Bake at 350°F/180°C/Gas 4 for 20 minutes.

Sounds rather extraordinary but is delicious!

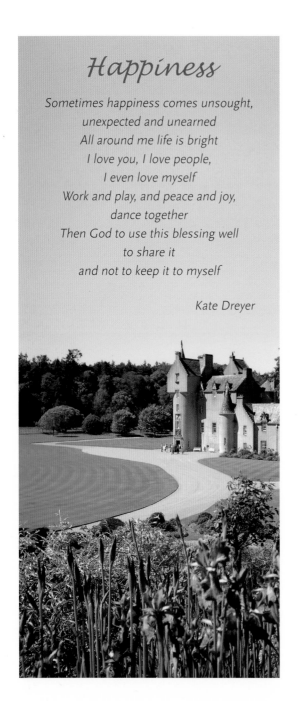

Happiness

Sometimes happiness comes unsought,
unexpected and unearned
All around me life is bright
I love you, I love people,
I even love myself
Work and play, and peace and joy,
dance together
Then God to use this blessing well
to share it
and not to keep it to myself

Kate Dreyer

Maple Syrup Chicken

(Serves 2)

INGREDIENTS

1 tablespoon olive oil
2 tablespoons maple syrup
1 crushed garlic clove
1 tablespoon grainy mustard
2 boneless chicken breasts
2 slices maple cured bacon

METHOD

Mix together in a bowl the oil, maple syrup, garlic and mustard. Place the chicken breasts in an oven-proof dish with the bacon on top and 3 tablespoons of cold water. Pour the mixture over and roast in the oven for 25 minutes at 400°F/200°C/Gas 6. Serve with potato dauphinois and a green vegetable.

This is the epitomy of taste, ease and speed

Aberdeen Angus is the best.
The pedigree herd was started
by my great-grandfather,
Sir George Macpherson-Grant
of Ballindalloch, in 1860. It is
now the oldest herd in existence.

Beef

Ballindalloch Beef Tournedos with a Whisky Cream Sauce

(Serves 2)

INGREDIENTS

2 Aberdeen Angus fillet steaks
about 1" (2.5cm) thick
2 rounds of fried bread
2 oz (50g) butter
1 finely chopped onion
4 oz (100g) sliced mushrooms
¼ pt (150ml) cream
1 tablespoon whisky
2 teaspoons chopped parsley
2 oz (50g) pâté

METHOD

Melt butter in pan and cook steaks until done as desired. Remove from pan and keep warm. Fry onion and mushrooms in pan with butter. Add whisky, cream, chopped parsley and seasoning. Simmer for few minutes. Spread fried bread round with pâté. Place beef on round and serve whisky sauce separately.

Showing our cattle at the Grantown Show.

A great treat and a must. One of my favourites

Ballindalloch Mince with a Crunchy Topping

(Serves 4)

INGREDIENTS

1 lb (450g) minced Aberdeen Angus beef
1 onion, chopped
2 tablespoons oil
Worcestershire and
  tomato sauces to taste
1 tablespoon plain flour
½ pt (300ml) beef stock

For the Topping:

4 oz (100g) butter (softened)
6 oz (150g) white breadcrumbs
2 oz (50g) grated parmesan cheese

For the Cheese Sauce:

1 oz (25g) butter (softened)
1 oz (25g) flour
½ pt (300ml) milk
2 oz (50g) grated strong cheese
1 egg yolk
Mix all ingredients together

METHOD

Gently fry onion in oil. Sprinkle with flour and allow to colour. Add mince and cook over gentle heat for 5-10 minutes. Add stock, sauces and seasoning to taste. Simmer stirring occasionally for 20 minutes. Meanwhile make cheese sauce. Place butter and flour and milk in pan whisk madly till thick. Add egg yolk and cheese. Pour mince into fireproof dish. Cool a little. Cover with cheese sauce. Make topping. Cut butter into small pieces, rub into breadcrumbs, add grated parmesan cheese and sprinkle on top. Place in hot oven 350°F/180°C/Gas 4 for 15 minutes.

Plain Roast Fillet of Aberdeen Angus Beef with Horseradish Sauce

(Serves 4)

INGREDIENTS

1 Fillet of Beef

**For the Horseradish &
Crème Fraîche Sauce:**

7 fl oz (200ml) crème fraîche
4 tablespoons M&S horseradish sauce
2 tablespoons mayonnaise
2 teaspoons Dijon mustard
chopped fresh parsley

*Plain, simple and superb
if the fillet of beef is
Aberdeen Angus!*

METHOD

Tie fillet to keep shape and roast at
10 minutes to the pound in oven
400°F/200°C/Gas 6 dotted with butter
and seasoning. I always check it by slicing
a small bit off the end and possibly a half
slice into middle to check it is slightly
pink still. When ready take out of oven
and rest for 5 minutes.

**For the Horseradish &
Crème Fraîche Sauce:**

Mix all the ingredients together and serve a
'blob' on the side of the plate.

Fillet of Aberdeen Angus en Croûte with Béarnaise Sauce

(Serves 4-6)

INGREDIENTS

1 lb 12 oz (750g) fillet of
 Aberdeen Angus beef
12 oz (350g) wild and cultivated
 mushrooms, finely chopped
1 oz (25g) butter
2 shallots, finely chopped
squeeze of lemon juice
2 tablespoons flat leaf parsley
1 packet chestnuts (chopped)
14 oz (400g) puff pastry
1 tablespoon Dijon mustard
1 medium egg (lightly beaten)
seasoning

METHOD

Fry shallot and finely sliced mushrooms in butter till translucent. Transfer to bowl. Stir in chopped chestnuts, parsley and lemon juice. Season and cool. Brush fillet with oil. Season and seal for 5 minutes each side in pan. Transfer to plate and cool. Roll out pastry thinly on floured work surface. Spread mushroom mixture down middle of pastry length. Brush top of fillet with mustard and place down on top of mushroom mixture. Parcel the fillet up, paint one of the long edges with beaten egg and both of the short sides. Parcel together, trim and cut away excess pastry. Place sealed edges down on roasting tin. Use pastry trimmings to decorate top and brush all over with beaten egg. Bake at 425°F/220°C/Gas 8 for about 30 minutes till golden. Leave to rest for 10 minutes. Meanwhile make Béarnaise sauce.

Champion Ebony

For the Béarnaise Sauce:

4 tablespoons white wine vinegar
2 shallots finely chopped
2 egg yolks
3 oz (75g) butter softened
seasoning
fresh tarragon
parsley
bunch of mixed herbs

For the Béarnaise Sauce:

Place vinegar, shallots and tarragon in pan. Bring to boil and reduce to 1 tablespoon. Cool. Then strain. Beat egg yolks and reduced vinegar. Place bowl over pan of simmering water and whisk for 3-4 minutes till pale and thickening. Beat in butter (small piece at a time) till sauce thickens. DO NOT BOIL. When thick take off heat and season and add finely chopped herbs. Serve with the fillet of Aberdeen Angus en croute.

Aberdeen-Angus Mince Cobbler

(Serves 4)

INGREDIENTS

1½ lb (675g). Aberdeen-Angus mince
1 onion finely chopped
2 tablespoon oil
Worcestershire and
  tomato sauces to taste
1 tablespoon plain flour
¾ pt (400ml) beef stock.

For the Cobbler:
6 oz (125 g) self raising flour
Pinch salt
1 tablespoon thyme and rosemary
4 oz (100 g) Chilled butter
  in small pieces
4 oz (100g) grated cheddar cheese
Juice of 1 lemon
1 egg lightly beaten for glaze

*A good winter
family lunch*

METHOD

Heat oil in large pan. Add onions. Sprinkle with flour and allow to colour. Add mince and cook over gentle heat for 5-10 minutes. Add stock, sauces and seasoning to taste. Simmer stirring occasionally for 20 minutes. Meanwhile make cobblers.

Tip flour, baking powder, salt, and herbs into large bowl. Add butter and rub in. Add cheddar cheese. Make a well, add lemon juice and 4 tablespoons of water. Gently mix together to make crumbly dough. Roll out onto floured surface to ¾" thick. Cut into 4-6 rounds using a 3" (7cm) cutter. Put mince into deep gratin dish and arrange cobbler around it. Brush with beaten egg. Place in oven and cook at 350°F/180°C/Gas 4 for 20 minutes till golden brown.

Fillet of Aberdeen Angus Pie

(Serves 4)

INGREDIENTS

1½ lb (675g) fillet of Aberdeen Angus
  beef or good stewing steak

1 onion peeled and finely sliced

2 oz (50g) unsalted butter

8 oz (225g) mushrooms, finely sliced
  (wild or porcini)

3 tablespoons brandy or whisky (optional)

1 teaspoon French mustard

3 tablespoons crème fraîche

3 fl oz (85ml) double cream

1 tablespoon tarragon finely chopped

paprika to taste

parsley for decoration

For the Pastry:

4 oz (100g) butter

6 oz (175g) plain flour

1 egg beaten + 1 egg to wash pastry

METHOD

Cut fillet into small chunks. Heat half
of butter in heavy based frying pan, add
onion and fry gently until soft and golden.
Remove with a slotted spoon and set
aside. Increase heat and quickly fry meat
in batches, set aside and keep warm.
Place all ingredients in pan. Lower heat
and stir in mustard, crème fraîche and
cream. Then place in round pie dish, roll
out pastry and cover. Place in oven at
350°F/180°C/Gas 4 for 20-30 minutes.
Serve with creamy mashed potatoes.

For the Pastry:

Rub flour and butter till looks like
breadcrumbs. Add beaten egg and mix
in (it will be sticky) place in fridge for 10
minutes. Roll out and place on pie dish.

Heats up well

Pork & Ham

Baked Glazed Ham with Fresh Peaches, Nectarines or Plums or Apricots

(Serves 6-8)

INGREDIENTS

4 lbs (1.8kg) middle cut gammon
bay leaves
1 onion stuck with cloves
½ pt (300ml) white wine
6 peppercorns
1½ oz (40g) demerara sugar
3½ fl oz (100ml) orange juice
2 tablespoons honey (thick)
1 tablespoon Dijon or coarse mustard
peaches and nectarines

For the Cumberland Sauce:

1 orange
1 lemon
4 tablespoons redcurrant jelly
4 tablespoons port
1 teaspoon mustard
seasoning
serve with fruit that is used above

METHOD

Soak ham in cold water overnight. Drain water off and cover with 8 fl oz (225ml) fresh water with onion, bay leaf and peppercorns, bring to boil cover and simmer for 30 minutes. Remove joint from pan. Take skin off ham. Score fat into diamond pattern and stud with cloves. Mix brown sugar, 2 tablespoons orange juice, mustard and 2 tablespoons honey together and brush thickly over ham. Place ham in oven with rest of wine and orange juice and baste with the honey glaze regularly. Bake at 400°F/200°C/Gas 6 for 1-1½ hours. To serve slice and surround with fresh peaches or nectarines, plums or apricots. Serve with Cumberland Sauce.

For the Cumberland Sauce:

Place juice from orange and lemon, redcurrant jelly and mustard in pan and heat slowly until dissolved. Simmer for 5 minutes. Add fruit. (as above optional)

Lovely Sunday Lunch

Collops of Pork Tenderloin with Meaux Mustard

(Serves 6)

INGREDIENTS

1 lb (450g) pork tenderloin
  cut into half inch discs
2 onions (sliced finely)
2 tablespoons Meaux mustard
2 fl oz (50ml) dry sherry
2 tablespoons olive oil
7 fl oz (200ml) crème fraîche
seasoning

METHOD

Sauté onions in large frying pan with olive oil till transparent. Remove onion with slotted spoon, then heat oil to highest setting. Add pork and stir fry for a few minutes. Add onions, sherry, mustard and crème fraîche. Simmer until sauce thickens. Season and serve with hot buttered noodles.

Clare's Pork

(Serves 6)

INGREDIENTS

8 pork chops
1 large finely chopped onion
1 pt (600ml) cream
4 tablespoons tomato purée
8 slices ham
8 dessertspoons grated cheese

METHOD

Fry pork chops gently in butter on both sides till golden brown. Place in a flat dish and cover with a slice of ham. Fry onion in butter and place on top of ham. Then sprinkle thickly with grated cheese. Pour tomato purée into pan with juices, fold in cream and season. Heat and pour over pork. Place in a moderate oven 350°F/180°C/Gas 4 for 20-25 minutes. Serve with brown rice and a green salad.

So easy, so delicious

Ham & Asparagus Gratin

(Serves 6)

INGREDIENTS

12 plump asparagus spears
6 slices honey roast ham (halved)
1½ oz (40g) butter
1½ oz (40g) flour
¾ pt (450ml) milk
2 teaspoons grainy mustard
3 oz (75g) gruyére cheese (grated)
pinch nutmeg
1 oz (25g) finely chopped
    parmesan cheese
1 oz (25g) white breadcrumbs

METHOD

Trim woody ends from asparagus, place in large frying pan with about 1 inch boiling water. Cover pan and cook for 4 minutes. Drain. Roll each asparagus spear in roast ham. Place in oven-proof dish. Melt butter in pan, add flour, cook for 1 minute stirring. Add milk, whisk like mad and bring to boil. Stir mustard, gruyére, seasoning and pinch of nutmeg into mixture. Pour sauce over asparagus and ham. Mix parmesan cheese with breadcrumbs and sprinkle over top. Bake for about 20 minutes at 350°F/180°C/Gas 4.

A perfect supper dish

Roast Rack of Pork
with Prune, Apple &
Apricot Stuffing

(Serves 4)

INGREDIENTS

4 lb (1.75 Kg) (6-rib) Pork Loin joint –
  As your butcher to score the skin

For the stuffing:

1 oz butter
1 leek (white part, diced)
1 shallot (diced)
2 cox apples (peeled and diced)
8 prunes and 8 apricots halved
  (preferably soaked)
pinch cinnamon and ginger
seasoning

For the gravy:

glass wine
½ pt (300ml) stock or water
2 tablespoons of gravy granules
  or cornflour

METHOD

Make a pocket through the centre of the loin with a sharp knife (you can ask your butcher to do this) to allow you to stuff the pork.

Prepare the stuffing by sweating the leek, shallot, apple, dried fruits and spices in the melted butter for several minutes. Allow to cool, and pack into pork loin pocket tightly. Tie with butcher's twine. Rub the skin with oil and salt. Place on a trivet in roasting pan, roast for first 30 minutes in a hot oven 400°F/200°C/Gas 6. Reduce temperature to 350°F/180°C/Gas 4 and roast for a further 2 hours. (As a guide cook pork joints for 30 minutes per 1 lb (450g) plus 30 minutes extra).

Remove joint from oven and rest in a warm place for 20 minutes before cutting string and carving.

For perfect crackling, cut off the string and cut away the crackling. Place on a baking tray, inner side uppermost and place back in a really hot oven for about 15 minutes until really crispy.

To make the gravy, top off any fat from the trivet, and place roasting tin directly on stove. Add the gravy granules or cornflour, the glass of wine and the stock or water. Bring it up to the boil. Simmer for a few minutes until it thickens. Pour into a pot, through a fine sieve. Serve with your carved pork, roast potatoes and vegetables.

Spicy Pork Chops

(Serves 4)

INGREDIENTS

4 pork chops
2 cloves garlic (peeled and crushed)
2 tablespoons Worcestershire sauce
2 tablespoons tomato purée
2 tablespoons lemon juice
3 tablespoons grainy mustard
3 tablespoons runny honey

METHOD

Brush chops with a little oil and fry them on both sides till golden brown. Place in oven-proof dish. Mix rest of ingredients together in bowl. Pour over chops and bake at 400°F/200°C/Gas 6 for about 30 minutes, basting occasionally. Remove from dish and serve with hot buttered pasta and a green vegetable.

Good supper dish

Pork Chops with Stilton Cheese or Gorgonzola

(Serves 4)

INGREDIENTS

4 large boneless pork loin chops
1 tablespoon olive oil
1 tablespoon green pesto
3 small tomatoes, thinly sliced
4 oz (110g) stilton or gorgonzola cheese
    cut into 4 thick slices
seasoning

Dead easy and tasty

METHOD

Brush chops with olive oil and season. Lay chops on baking sheet and grill for 4-5 minutes on both sides. Remove from grill and brush both each one with pesto. Place tomato slices on top then add cheese, Place chops under the grill again for 2-4 minuted until cheese is bubbling and melted. Serve with couscous and a herby salad.

Pork Stroganoff

(Serves 4-6)

Very easy and can wait!

INGREDIENTS

2 lbs (900g) pork fillet
1 teaspoon honey
1 packet chestnuts
seasoning
2 large onions
6 oz (175g) mushrooms
2 teaspoons paprika
2 tablespoons flour
2 tablespoons oil
3½ fl oz (100ml) sherry
½ pt (300ml) Full fat crème fraîche
Juice of ½ lemon

METHOD

Cut pork fillet into strips and roll into honey. Season. Fry pork quickly in oil over high heat. Set aside on plate. Melt knob of butter in pan, add finely sliced onion and fry for a few minutes till translucent. Add sliced mushrooms and chopped chestnuts and fry gently for few minutes. Sprinkle in paprika. Add sherry and crème fraîche, bring to boil stirring and allow to thicken. Season. Return pork to pan, add lemon juice and heat through for 2 minutes. Serve with hot rice.

Lamb

Rack of Banffshire Lamb with a Herb Crust & Mint Hollandaise sprinkled with Streaky Bacon

(Serves 4)

INGREDIENTS

2 racks best end French-trimmed lamb
  – 6 ribs/ 11 oz (300g) each
1 tablespoon olive oil
2 tablespoons Dijon mustard
  (for sticking herb crust to the lamb)
streaky bacon (fried and chopped)

For the Herb Crust:

3 oz (75g) dried white breadcrumbs
2 tablespoons chopped parsley
1 teaspoon chopped thyme
1 teaspoon chopped rosemary
1 tablespoon lemon oil
1 clove garlic crushed (optional)

For the Mint Hollandaise:

4 egg yolks
1 tablespoon water
2 tablespoons lemon juice
6 oz (150g) melted butter
seasoning
1 tablespoon chopped mint

METHOD

Whizz herb crust ingredients for a few seconds in food processor or mix in bowl.

Heat the olive oil in frying pan and sear the lamb over a hot heat until lightly browned on both sides. Spread with mustard and press crumb mixture on top. Place racks on wire trivet and roast in hot oven for 15-20 minutes at 425°F/220°C/Gas 7 depending on how pink you like your lamb. Sprinkle with chopped bacon and serve with Mint Hollandaise.

For the mint Hollandaise:

Whisk egg yolks, water and lemon juice in bowl over a hot water. Pour in hot melted butter and whisk until thick. Season and add mint.

My favourite of all Main Courses

Loin of Lamb en Croûte with Mangoes & Chestnuts

(Serves 4)

INGREDIENTS

2 fillets of Scottish lamb –
  about 7 oz (200g) each
6 oz (175g) finely chopped mushrooms
8 oz (225g) coarse country pâté
2-3 tablespoons olive oil
1 tin mangoes (strained and chopped)
  plus extra for decoration
1 small packet chopped chestnuts
2 x 13 oz (375g) packets of ready-rolled
  puff pastry
8 oz (225g) large spinach leaves
1 large egg, beaten
1 garlic clove, finely chopped
seasoning

METHOD

Heat 2 tablespoons olive oil in frying pan.
Sear lamb fillets all over till browned.
Remove from pan and set aside. Fry
mushrooms and garlic lightly. Remove
from pan with slotted spoon and set
aside. Mix together pâté, mushrooms,
garlic, chopped mangoes and chestnuts.
Season. Wash spinach leaves and place
in saucepan. Cook gently till wilted.
Squeeze water out well. Cool. Place ready-
rolled pieces of puff pastry on board.
Lay spinach leaves on top. Spread pâté
mixture over top of spinach, then place
fillets of lamb on each piece of pâté, and
fold down middle into two neat parcels.
Brush with beaten egg and place on
baking tray. Rest in fridge for 10 minutes,
then bake at 400°F/200°C/Gas 6 for
20-25 minutes till pastry is crusty and
golden. Serve sliced thickly with some
warmed slices of mango on the side.

Sensational – melts in the mouth

The kiss of the sun for
pardon, the song of the
birds for mirth
One is nearer God's
heart in a garden than
anywhere else on earth

Noisettes of Lamb on a Bed of Pea Purée with Mint Hollandaise

(Serves 4)

INGREDIENTS

8 noisettes of lamb
   (get butcher to do them)
8 rounds of fried bread
hollandaise sauce
8 field mushrooms
butter

For the Pea Purée:

14 oz (400g) frozen peas
mint leaves
2 oz (50ml) double cream
seasoning

For the Mint Hollandaise:

4 egg yolks
1 tablespoon water
2 tablespoons lemon juice
1 tablespoon finely chopped mint
6 oz (150g) melted butter
seasoning

METHOD

Deep fry rounds of bread in butter. Lay aside and keep warm. Fry mushrooms in butter. Lay aside and keep warm. Fry the noisettes in butter for about 3-4 minutes on each side. Place on fried bread with mushrooms on top. Serve with mint hollandaise on a bed of pea purée.

For the Pea Purée:

Cook peas in salted boiling water for about 4-6 minutes. Liquidise peas. Add cream and season.

For the Mint Hollandaise:

Whisk egg yolks, water and lemon juice in bowl over hot water. Pour in slowly melted butter and whisk until thick. Season and add chopped mint.

P.S. If it curdles, add an ice cube and whisk like mad!

Stylish

Leg of Lamb Stuffed with Spinach, Prunes & Chestnuts

(Serves 4)

INGREDIENTS

1 x 6 lb (2.7kg) leg of lamb (boned)
1 packet 10 oz (275g) creamed spinach
  (frozen at Waitrose)
1 tin prunes
1 small onion (grated)
1 packet chestnuts
2 tablespoons fresh breadcrumbs
1 grated lemon
seasoning
root vegetables

METHOD

Chop prunes and chestnuts, then add defrosted creamed spinach, grated onion, breadcrumbs, grated lemon and seasoning. Stuff lamb with mixture and sew up. Roast for about 2 hours in oven at 375°F/190°C/Gas 5 on a layer of root vegetables.

Herby Lamb Cutlets with Soubise Sauce

(Serves 4)

INGREDIENTS
8 French trimmed lamb cutlets
3 large eggs beaten
4 oz (100g) fresh white breadcrumbs
1 teaspoon rosemary
2 tablespoons chopped fresh parsley
1 teaspoon thyme
2 oz (25g) butter
1 tablespoon grated parmesan cheese
4 tablespoons Vegetable oil
1 grated lemon

For the Soubise Sauce:
2 oz (25g) butter
2 onions (thinly sliced)
3½ fl oz (100ml) double cream
1 bay leaf
pinch of cayenne
seasoning

METHOD
Place cutlets on baking parchment and flatten nwith rolling pin. Season. Put eggs (beaten) in bowl and then mix together the bread, Rosemary, chopped parsley, thyme, parmesan, grated lemon and seasoning. Dip each cutlet into first the egg and then into herb mixture. Flatten with rolling pin. Chill for a few hours. Meanwhile make soubise sauce.

Heat butter in pan. Add finely sliced onion and cook on low heat till translucent. Add cream, seasoning and cayenne. Warm through gently and then liquidize till smooth. Keep warm.

Heat butter and oil in pan and fry cutlets for 2-3 minutes on each side. Serve with a blob of Soubise and green vegetables.

I think of Heaven as a garden
where I shall find again
my dear ones who have made my world.

Venison & Game

Ballindalloch Venison Casserole with Plums or Blackberries & Chestnuts

(Serves 4)

INGREDIENTS

2 lbs (900g) venison or roe deer
  cut into 1in (2.5cm) cubes
3-4 tablespoons sunflower oil
2 onions, skinned and finely sliced
1 pt (600ml) game stock
1 tablespoon redcurrant jelly
¼ pt (150ml) port or red wine
1 x 15 oz (425g) tin whole chestnuts
  (halved)
1 lb (450g) Victoria plums
  (stoned and quartered) or blackberries
2 tablespoons seasoned flour
seasoning

METHOD

Toss cubed venison in two tablespoons seasoned flour. Heat oil in pan and fry meat till brown. Take out of pan and leave. Add sliced onions to pan and cook till soft. Replace meat into pan with onions stir in stock, redcurrant jelly, wine, chestnuts and plums/blackberries. Stir till boiling point, then place in casserole and cook at 350°F/180°C/Gas 4 for 1 hour. Serve with creamed potatoes and mixture of roasted vegetables.

Venison Wellington

(Serves 6)

INGREDIENTS

2 lb (900g) venison or roe deer fillet
2 teaspoons brandy
3 oz (75g) butter
1 onion (finely chopped)
3 oz (75g) sliced mushrooms
1 large packet puff pastry
3 oz (75g) pâté (you can buy
   farmhouse pâté at most supermarkets)
1 egg lightly beaten
seasoning
thyme

METHOD

Season the venison. Melt butter in heavy frying pan. Add meat, turning to seal fully. Flame brandy and remove from pan. Fry onion and mushrooms in pan, add thyme and cook gently till liquids have evaporated. Cool. Roll out puff pastry to large oblong. Mix together pâté and mushroom mixture and spread down middle of pastry. Place venison fillet on top. Fold up pastry like parcel and seal ends. Place venison on baking tray and brush with beaten egg. Bake at 400°F/200°C/Gas 6 for 20 minutes.

Venison, Mushroom & Red Wine Pie

(Serves 4-6)

INGREDIENTS

2 oz (50g) butter
2 large onions
1 tablespoon redcurrant jelly
9 oz (250g) mushrooms (sliced)
3 tablespoons flour
3 lb (1.5kg) diced fillet of venison
½ pt (500ml) beef stock
½ pt (500ml) red wine
2 sprigs of fresh thyme
13 oz (375g) ready rolled shortcrust pastry
1 beaten egg to glaze pastry

METHOD

Heat butter in large casserole dish (with lid), add onions and finely chopped mushrooms. Cook gently for 15 minutes till soft, then stir in flour and cook for 2 minutes. Add venison, season and cook for five minutes. Add stock, wine and thyme. Bring to simmer for few minutes. Cool completely and transfer to pie dish. Place pastry on floured service. Cut off a couple of strips to line lip of pie dish. Brush with beaten egg and lay pastry sheet on top. Chill for twenty minutes. Cut steam hole in middle and bake for 30-40 minutes at 350°F/180°C/gas 4. Serve with potato dauphinois and green vegetables.

Such a natural and lean meat

Crusty Loin of Venison

(Serves 4)

INGREDIENTS
1 loin of venison
2 tablespoons olive oil
2 tablespoons dijon mustard or 1 egg (beaten)
fried streaky bacon

For the Herb Crust:
3 oz (75g) white breadcrumbs
2 tablespoons chopped parsley
1 teaspoon chopped thyme
1 teaspoon chopped rosemary
1 tablespoon olive oil
1 tablespoon grated parmesan

METHOD
Whizz herb crust ingredients for few seconds in food processor or mix in bowl. Slice venison filet (having taken off any fat) in 1" collops, flatten a little with rolling pin. Heat olive oil in frying pan and fry the venison over hot heat till lightly browned on both sides. Spread with mustard or beaten egg and press crumb mixture all over. Place collops on trivet and roast for 15-20 minutes at 425°F/220°C/Gas 7. Serve sprinkled with bacon and a blob of rowan jelly or hollandaise.

Fillet of Roe Deer Sprinkled with Roasted Flaked Almonds & Served with a Port & Nectarine Sauce

(Serves 4-6)

INGREDIENTS

1 boned saddle of roe deer
  (ask butcher to bone)
3 tablespoons olive oil
knob of butter
seasoning
flour
4 oz (100g) almond flakes

For the Port and Nectarine Sauce:

5 nectarines
4 tablespoons port
2 tablespoons redcurrant jelly
1 tablespoon Worcestershire sauce
2 oz (50g) butter
rind and juice of 1 orange
seasoning

METHOD

Make sauce first by placing all ingredients (except nectarines) in pan. Reduce liquid by simmering for about 15 minutes. Season, add 4 sliced nectarines, keep warm. Heat oil and butter in frying pan. Take skin (if there is any) off fillets. Quickly roll venison in seasoned flour and fry for 2-3 minutes (for rare) on each side of both loins. Place on hot serving plate and keep warm. Brown flaked almonds quickly in hot oven. Slice fillets diagonally and sprinkle almonds over venison. Pour sauce around venison and decorate with extra nectarine. Serve with creamed potatoes.

Tender and succulant

Pheasant Nuggets with Home-Made Tomato Sauce

(Serves 4)

INGREDIENTS

5 pheasant breasts, cut into thin strips
⅓ loaf of white bread
  (made into breadcrumbs)
seasoned flour
1 teaspoon paprika
2 eggs, beaten
1 tablespoon sunflower oil

For the home-made Tomato Sauce:
2 tablespoons olive oil
1 finely chopped onion
1 x 15 oz (450g) tin of tomatoes
Sugar to taste
teaspoon of Lea & Perrins
seasoning
a pinch of fresh basil
  or finely chopped parsley

METHOD

Heat oil in frying pan. Dust strips of pheasant in flour. Dip into beaten egg and then into breadcrumbs (seasoned and with a pinch of paprika). Fry the nuggets gently until crispy and golden. Serve with fried sliced potatoes and accompany with home-made tomato sauce.

For the home-made Tomato Sauce:
Fry finely chopped onion in oil. Add tomatoes. Liquidise. Season. Add sugar and Lea & Perrins to taste. Serve warm or cold.

Bluebelle with a pheasant

Wild Duck with Orange & Blackberry Sauce

(Serves 4)

INGREDIENTS
2 wild ducks
1 orange
knob butter

For the Sauce:
1 onion (finely sliced)
2 tablespoons oil
2 cloves garlic (peeled and chopped
1 punnet blackberries
1 teaspoon freshly grated root ginger
1 dessertspoon redcurrant jelly
large dash soy sauce
seasoning
juice and zest of 1 orange

METHOD
Place ½ orange in both ducks and rub all over with butter. Place ducks in tin with tablespoon of water. Roast at 400°F/200°C/Gas 6 for 15 minutes – they should still be pink inside. Meanwhile, make sauce. Heat oil and fry onions and garlic. Stir in blackberries and cook until soft. Add grated ginger, sugar, orange and soy sauce. Stir, season and keep warm. Slice breasts of duck and place on hot dish and cover with spicy sauce.

They are the best if young birds

Wild Duck with Marmalade Sauce

(Serves 4)

INGREDIENTS

2 wild duck
6 oz (175g) home-made marmalade
1 glass red wine/port
5 fl oz (150ml) orange juice
5 fl oz (150ml) strong chicken stock
5 fl oz (150ml) crème fraîche
1 orange

METHOD

Sprinkle ducks with salt. Place in roasting tin with glass of wine/port and knob of butter inside them. Roast at 400°F/200°C/Gas 6 for 15-20 minutes. Meanwhile make sauce. Place marmalade, orange juice, stock and sugar in pan over heat and bring to boil. Simmer for 10 minutes. Season and stir in crème fraîche. Bring to boil again and keep warm. Slice ducks and place on oven-proof plate. Pour sauce around them and decorate with sliced fresh oranges.

Passion for Puddings

Strawberry Cheesecake with Raspberries

(Serves 2)

INGREDIENTS

3 digestive biscuits
5 oz (150g) full fat soft cheese
2 fl oz (50ml) double cream
1 tablespoon caster sugar
8 oz (225g) strawberry punnet
small punnet raspberries for decoration
2 leaves gelatine

METHOD

Place 2 x 3½" (9cm) metal rings on 2 small desert plates. Liquidise digestive biscuits till like fine breadcrumbs and divide between the rings kneading into the rings to make a base. Liquidise strawberries, add melted gelatine (with water squeezed out) and mix into soft cheese and double cream. Spoon mixture into rings and flatten top. Chill for 4 hours or more. Decorate with raspberries.

Easy Peasy Chocolate Mousse

(Serves 6)

INGREDIENTS

4 oz (100g) milk chocolate
2 oz (50g) plain chocolate
few drops vanilla essence
1 chocolate Cadbury flake
pouring cream or bowl of crème fraîche
3 eggs (separated)

METHOD

Melt chocolate in bowl over hot water. Cool. Add egg yolks one at a time and beat in well. Beat egg whites till stiff, then fold in the chocolate with metal spoon. Put in fridge for couple of hours. To serve sprinkle all over with Cadbury flake or top with chocolate profiteroles. Serve with jug of pouring cream or bowl of crème fraîche.

Everybody loves this - always a winner

The Three Snows

(Serves 4-6)

INGREDIENTS
1 lb (450g) apples
1 egg white
¼ pt (150ml) double cream
¼ pt (150ml) crème fraîche
  or plain Greek yoghurt
sugar to taste

METHOD
Peel, core and slice apples. Place in pan with tablespoon of water and tablespoon sugar. Cook till soft. Liquidise apples and place in bowl. Cool. Whip cream till soft peaks. Fold in crème fraîche. Add apple purée to cream mixture, then fold in whisked egg whites. Before serving sprinkle with crushed brandy snap or brown sugar.

P.S. To make other flavours, for example, gooseberry and rhubarb just swap the fruits. For Strawberry and Raspberry just blitz and then follow recipe.

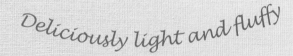

Deliciously light and fluffy

Diana's Syrup with Apple Sponge

(Serves 6-8)

INGREDIENTS

2 cored, peeled and sliced apples
4 oz (100g) butter
4 oz (100g) caster sugar
6 oz (150g) self-raising flour, sifted
2 eggs, beaten
few drops vanilla flavouring
a little milk to mix
1 small tin golden syrup

METHOD

Half fill a large saucepan with water and put it on to boil. Grease a 1½ pt (900ml) pudding basin and put the cored, peeled and sliced apples at bottom of basin. Pour in 2 tablespoons of golden syrup. Cream together butter and sugar until pale and fluffy. Add beaten eggs and a few drops vanilla essence a little at a time. Fold in half the sifted flour, then fold in the rest. Add a little milk, approximately 3 tablespoons to give a dropping consistency. Pour mixture into greased basin, cover with greaseproof paper and secure with string. Stand bowl in large saucepan half-filled with boiling water and boil with lid on for about 1½ hours. Turn out and serve with the rest of the golden syrup (warmed).

Lovely Lemon Pudding

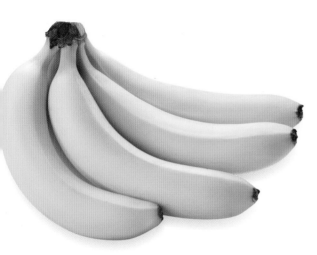

(Serves 4)

INGREDIENTS
6 oz (170g) granulated sugar
1 tablespoon self-raising flour
½ oz (15g) butter
2 eggs
2 lemons, grated and squeezed
scant ½ pt (300ml) milk

METHOD
Oven temperature 350°F/180°C/Gas 4
Butter 6 cocotte dishes (ovenproof). Rub
butter into the flour and mix in sugar.
Separate the eggs and whip the whites.
Mix yolks together with grated lemon rind
and juice and stir into the dry mixture.
Add milk gradually, stirring well. Finally
fold in the beaten egg whites and bake
in the prepared
dishes in oven
for about 25
minutes or
until the top
is golden
brown and
firm.

Banana Cream

(Serves 4)

INGREDIENTS
2 tablespoons crème fraîche
¼ pt (150ml) double cream
4 bananas
sugar to taste
crumbled chocolate flake
1 squeeze lemon

METHOD
Squash Bananas well with fork, sprinkle
with lemon juice. Whip cream, add crème
fraîche, fold in bananas. Sprinkle with
chocolate flake.

Poached Pear with Clotted Cream & Honey Ice Cream

(Serves 4)

INGREDIENTS

4 large desert pears
5 oz (150g) caster sugar
¼ pt (150ml) red wine
¼ pt (150ml) water

For the Clotted Cream & Honey Ice Cream:

1 jar (150ml) clotted cream
½ pt (300ml) double cream
1 tin condensed milk
2½ fl oz (60ml) honey

METHOD

Peel pears with potato peeler leaving stalk on. Put sugar, wine and water in pan, heat gently till dissolved. Bring to boil and simmer for 2 minutes. Put pears upright in syrup. Cover and simmer for 15 minutes until pears are soft. Transfer each one to plate, pour a little wine sauce over top and serve with clotted cream and honey ice cream.

For the Clotted Cream & Honey Ice Cream:

Mix clotted cream and double cream together. Add condensed milk and honey. Place in deep freeze. Take out 15–20 minutes before serving.

Apple Crumble

(Serves 4)

INGREDIENTS

1-1½ lbs (675g) apples
1 lb (450g) plums (stoned)
juice of 1 lemon
3 oz (75g) caster sugar or to taste

For the Crumble Topping:

4 oz (100g) butter
8 oz (225g) brown sugar
5 oz (150g) plain flour
1 teaspoon ground cinnamon

METHOD

Peel and slice apples and par cook. Add halved plums and warm till soft, mix well. Sprinkle on baked topping and place in oven at 350°F/180°C/ Gas 4 for about 15 minutes.

For the Crumble Topping:

Place all dry ingredients in bowl and mix well. Tip onto baking tray and flatten with fork. Place in oven at 350°F/180°C/ Gas 4 for about 10 minutes.

Bertie and Caras favourite

Dark & White Chocolate Mousses Topped with a Profiterole

(Serves 6)

INGREDIENTS
For the White Chocolate Mousse:

3 oz (75g) greens organic white chocolate

3 oz (75g) Lindt white chocolate

2 eggs separated

INGREDIENTS
For the Dark Chocolate Mousse:

5 oz (150g) Cadburys milk chocolate

1 oz (25g) Bourneville dark chocolate

2 eggs separated

METHOD

Melt white chocolate in bowl over a pan of boiling water. Cool. Add egg yolks one by one and mix well. Beat egg whites till stiff. Fold into white chocolate mixture carefully. Pour mixture into 4 tea cups or 4 glass dishes and leave to set for 2-3 hours. Then melt milk chocolate and dark chocolate (as above), cool, beat in egg yolks. Beat egg whites till stiff. Fold into chocolate mixture carefully. Pour on top of set white chocolate. Leave until set and top with a profiterole.

George and Louisa love these

One for my desert island

Queen of Puddings

(Serves 4-6)

INGREDIENTS

¾ pt (450ml) milk
1 oz (25g) butter
grated rind of 1 lemon
2 eggs separated
4 oz (100g) caster sugar
3 oz (75g) fresh white breadcrumbs
6 tablespoons raspberry jam

METHOD

Place milk, butter and lemon rind in saucepan and heat gently. Whisk egg yolks with 1 oz (25g) sugar till pale and thick, then gradually whisk in hot milk mixture. Stir in breadcrumbs and pour into ovenproof dish. Leave to stand for 15 minutes. Bake at 325°F/170°C/Gas 3 for 30 minutes. Remove from oven and spread lightly with jam. Whisk egg whites till stiff then gradually add 3 oz (75g) sugar. Spoon mixture over pudding and bake for further 15 minutes or until meringue is set.

This must be one of the oldest recipes - it was made popular by Queen Charlotte. Her Majesty considered it a nutritious and economical dish to serve patients at her hospital. To honour the Queen the meringue was piped around the sides to give an impression of a crown.

I had to add this again as it is such wonderful comfort food!

Mini Summer Puddings

(Serves 4)

INGREDIENTS
1 lb (450g) mixed red fruit
½ small loaf (white)
1 lb (450g) sugar
3 fl oz (75ml) water

METHOD
Roll white bread into thin
slices. Cut out 3 rounds for
each pudding with pastry cutter
and lids. Meanwhile place fruit in
pan with water and sugar. Heat gently.
Place first round in pastry cutter followed
by spoonful of fruit. Repeat once and
then place last round on top. Pour rest of
juice on top. Press top of pastry cutter
on firmly. Leave in fridge over night.
Then push lid down through cutter onto
plate and decorate with a strawberry.
Serve with double cream or ice cream

Ballindalloch Golden Syrup Tart with Clotted Cream Ice Cream

(Serves 4-6)

INGREDIENTS

For the Pastry:

5 oz (150g) butter in pieces
8 oz (225g) plain flour
1 egg yolk
2 tablespoons (30ml) cold water
1 dessertspoon caster sugar

For the Filling:

1½ lb (700g) tin golden syrup
6 oz (175g) fresh white breadcrumbs
grated rind and juice of 3 lemon
2 eggs lightly beaten

METHOD

Make pastry, put flour and butter in liquidiser and whizz till mixture resembles breadcrumbs. Add egg yolk, sugar and 2 tablespoons cold water, whizz briefly to firm dough. Turn onto floured board and knead lightly. Wrap in cling film and chill for 30 minutes. Roll pastry out onto floured surface and line a 10 inch (25cm) loose based cake tin 1½" (4cm) deep. Prick the base with fork. Bake blind at 350°F/180°C/Gas 4 for 20 minutes.

For the filling, lightly heat golden syrup in pan. Remove from heat and fold in breadcrumbs and lemon zest. Stir in eggs. Pour into pastry case and bake at 350°F/180°C/Gas 4 for 45-50 minutes till lightly set and golden. Serve with clotted cream ice cream.

Wonderful winter pudding

Apricot & Custard Tart

(Serves 6)

INGREDIENTS

For the Pastry:

4 oz (100g) butter

6 oz (150g) plain flour

1 teaspoon icing sugar

For the Filling:

6-8 apricots (fresh if possible)

½ pt (300ml) single cream

4 egg yolks

3 oz (75g) caster sugar

METHOD

Whizz pastry ingredients in processor till like fine breadcrumbs. Mould into 7" flan tin. Cool in fridge. Place on hot tray and bake at 350°F/180°C/Gas 4 for 20-25 minutes.

For the Filling:

Dip whole fresh apricots into boiling water. Skin, halve and stone. Beat together cream, egg yolks and sugar. Arrange halved apricots on pastry base and pour over custard mixture. Bake at 350°F/180°C/Gas 4 for 20-25 minutes until custard is set firm. Serve warm with whipped cream.

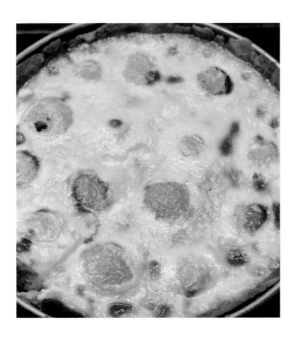

Delicious, plain and simple

Kenny's Very Special Banana Orange and Passion Fruit Soufflé

(Serves 6)

INGREDIENTS

2 bananas
1 orange (zest and juice)
6 passion fruits
1 tablespoon Grand Marnier or Cointreau
6 oz (175g) crème patisserie
6 large egg whites
2 oz (50g) caster sugar plus extra for dusting ramekins

(Crème patisserie or French pastry cream is used in many desserts including profiteroles)

6 egg yolks
4½ oz (115g) caster sugar
2½ oz (65g) plain flour
¾ pt (450ml) milk

METHOD

Whisk together sugar and egg yolks. Mix in the flour trying to avoid any lumps. Whisk in the boiling milk, return to the pan and cook out the custard for a minute or two until thickened. You can add a splash of vanilla essence at this stage if preferred. This will make more than you need for this recipe, but it is a useful thing to have in the fridge.

For the Soufflé:

Butter and sugar 6 ramekins. Halve the passion fruits and scoop the fruit into a pot with some of the orange zest and the orange juice. Add the liqueur. Simmer for 30 seconds and sieve into another pan to remove the passion fruit seeds. Add the chopped bananas and cook for several minutes further so that the banana goes soft and does not discolour. Blend the sauce or pass through the sieve one more time. Add 6 oz of the Pastry Cream and whisk to avoid lumps. You now have the base for your soufflé.

Oliver's favourite

At the top of my list for a desert island

Whisk the egg whites to soft peaks then gradually add the caster sugar and whisk until firm peaks are reached. Carefully fold through your soufflé base and fill the soufflé dishes with the soufflé mixture. Smooth the tops with a large spoon or palate knife and run round edge of the soufflé to push the mixture away from the edge. Cook the soufflé in a pre-heated oven at 400°F/200°C/Gas 6 for 10-12 minutes. Dust the tops with icing sugar and serve.

The Soufflé can be accompanied with a Passion Fruit Sauce. Recipe overleaf.

The Soufflé can be accompanied with a Passion Fruit Sauce.

INGREDIENTS
12 passion fruits
juice of 2 oranges
2 tablespoons orange liqueur
1 tablespoon icing sugar

METHOD
Scoop the passion fruit pulp into a pan with the other ingredients. Bring to the boil and simmer for 1 minute and then sieve.

Lemon Meringue Pie

(Serves 4-6)

INGREDIENTS

For the Pastry:

6 oz (150g) plain flour
pinch of salt
3 oz (75g) butter
1 egg yolk
1-2 tablespoon cold water

For the Filling:

3 oz (75g) butter
2 large lemons
½ lb (225g) sugar
3 eggs

For the Meringue:

3 egg whites
6 oz (150g) caster sugar

METHOD

Grease an 8" diameter flan tin.
Start by making the pastry. Sift the flour
and salt into bowl and rub in the butter
until it resembles fine breadcrumbs. Beat
egg yolk and add to centre of mixture.
Bind together with a little cold water
until you have a smooth ball of dough.
Wrap in cling film and refrigerate for
30 minutes. Then line the prepared flan
ring with baking paper and baking beans.
Bake for 10 minutes at 350°F/180°C/
Gas 4. Remove beans and paper. Bake
for further 5 minutes.

For the Filling:

Meanwhile put butter into double
saucepan, add sugar, juice of lemons
and the strained beaten eggs. Stir
constantly over moderate heat till thick.
Cool, pour into pastry case.

For the Meringue:

Beat egg whites with caster sugar till stiff
peaks. Place on top of filling. Put in oven
at 300°F/150°C/Gas 2 till meringue is
pale beige.

An old fashioned recipe which I love

Apple & Caramel Crumble

(Serves 4-6)

INGREDIENTS

1½ lbs (675g) cooking apples
2 oz (50g) butter
1 Tin Nestles condensed caramel sauce

For the Topping:

4 oz (100g) softened butter
8 oz (225g) soft brown sugar
5 oz (150g) plain flour
1 teaspoon ground cinnamon

De-licious.
The best crumble ever!

METHOD

Peel, core and slice apples into bowl. Tip into frying pan with 2 oz (50g) butter and fry gently till soft. Grease 2pt (1.2 ltr) ovenproof dish and tip apples in. Pour warmed caramel on top and place in oven 350°F/180°C/Gas 4 for about 15 minutes. Meanwhile place all dry ingredients in bowl and mix well. Put on to baking tray lined with foil, flatten gently with fork and place in oven at 350°F/180°C/Gas 4 for about 15 minutes – watch it like a hawk so it does not brown! Take out and tip on top of apple. Serve with double or clotted cream.

Hot Cross Bun, Bread & Butter Pudding

(Serves 6)

INGREDIENTS

6 hot cross buns
3 oz (75g) softened butter
finely grated zest of 2 oranges

INGREDIENTS

For the Custard:

½ pt (300ml) milk
1 pt (600ml) double cream
2 oz (50g) caster sugar
8 egg yolks
2 eggs

METHOD

Cut buns into 3 slices horizontally and spread both sides of each slice with butter. Place artistically in row in oven proof dish and sprinkle with zest of orange. Place cream and milk into large pan, bring to boil remove from heat. In large bowl whisk egg yolks and 2 whole eggs till light and fluffy. Then add hot cream mixture whisking well. Strain through sieve into pan cook over low heat stirring constantly till thickens and coats the back of wooden spoon. Pour custard over buns leave for 1 hour for buns to soak up custard. Bake pudding at 275°F/140°C/Gas 3 for 35 minutes till golden and bubbling. Sprinkle with demerara sugar and serve with double cream.

Wonderful nursery pudding which everyone adores

Upside Down Pear & Gingerbread Pudding served with a Salted Caramel Sauce

(Serves 6)

INGREDIENTS

4 oz (100g) butter
4 oz (100g) soft brown sugar
15 oz (425g) tin of pears in fruit juice
4 oz (100g) plain flour
half teaspoon bicarbonate of soda
2 teaspoon cinnamon
1 teaspoon ground ginger
Pinch nutmeg and cloves
1 egg lightly beaten
4 oz (100g) dark brown sugar
3 oz (75g) treacle
¼ pt (150ml) milk
double cream for serving

For the Caramel Sauce:

4 oz (100g) butter
6 oz (175g) soft brown sugar
½ pt (300ml) double cream
few drops vanilla essence
pinch of salt
caramel sauce

METHOD

Make topping first by melting 2 oz (50g) butter and soft brown sugar. Stir for 1-2 minutes over gentle heat. Pour into ovenproof dish 8" (20cm) diameter. Arrange sliced pears in fan shape over sauce. Sieve together into bowl the flour bicarbonate of soda, cinnamon, ginger, cloves and nutmeg. Melt remaining butter and mix in egg, dark brown sugar, treacle and milk. Stir into dry ingredients and mix well. Spoon mixture over pears. Smooth surface and bake at 350°F/180°C/ Gas 4 for 40-50 minutes. Remove from oven, leave to settle for 2 minutes and then turn out onto warm plate. Serve with Salted Caramel Sauce.

For the Caramel Sauce:

Place all ingredients in pan and bring to simmering. Serve.

Had to put this recipe in again as it is the "Best of Best"

Strawberry and Apple Meringue

(Serves 6)

INGREDIENTS

1 lb (450g) apples
   (peeled, cored and sliced)
½ lb (225g) strawberries
   (topped and cut in half)
1 tablespoon sugar

INGREDIENTS

For the Meringue topping:

2 egg whites
4 oz (100g) caster sugar

METHOD

Place apples in pan with a little water and sugar. Cook till soft. Add strawberries to soften. Cool. Place in serving dish or 6 large cocotte dishes. Beat egg whites till stiff, fold in caster sugar. Top apple and strawberry mixture with meringue and place in oven for about 3 minutes at 425°F/220°C/Gas 7. Then another 10 minutes at 300°F/150°C/Gas 2. Serve with clotted cream or strawberry ice cream.

When you have a glut of apples this is a different and delicious recipe

Black Cherry Pancakes

(Serves 4-6)

INGREDIENTS
For the Pancake Batter (makes 8):
4 oz (100g) flour
2 eggs
½ pt (300ml) milk
2 oz (50g) butter (melted)
pinch of salt

For the Filling:
1 x 15 oz (425g) tin of black cherries
  (stoned)
½ pt (300ml) double cream
2 tablespoons flaked
  and browned almonds

METHOD
Place flour, eggs, milk, salt and cooled melted butter in liquidiser and process till smooth. Stand in fridge for at least 10 minutes. Make the pancakes and fill with black cherries. Place in shallow dish and pour over cream. Put in moderate oven 350°F/180°C/Gas 4 for 15 minutes. Sprinkle with almonds.

Gooseberry & Apricot Crumble

(Serves 4)

INGREDIENTS
8 oz (225g) gooseberries
6 fresh apricots, or dried or tinned
2 tablespoons sugar

For the Topping:
4 oz (100g) softened butter
8 oz (225g) soft brown sugar
5 oz (150g) plain flour
1 teaspoon ground cinnamon

METHOD
Top and tail gooseberries and place in small amount of water with sugar. Bring to boil and cook till soft. Add apricots and warm all together. Place in oven-proof dish. Make topping and sprinkle over top. Place in oven for 5 minutes at 350°F/180°C/Gas 4.

For the Topping:
Place all dry ingredients in bowl and mix together until resembling breadcrumbs. Place on baking tray with foil. Place in oven at 350°F/180°C/Gas 4 for 10-15 minutes. Then sprinkle over the 'goosegogs'.

Raspberry & Blackberry Crème Brûlée

(Serves 6)

INGREDIENTS

1 punnet (150g) blackberries
1 punnet (150g) raspberries
8 egg yolks
1 pint (600ml) double cream
6 brandy snaps
sugar to taste

METHOD

Whisk egg yolks with 1 tablespoon of cream. Boil rest of the cream and pour over eggs. Pour into double saucepan whisk over simmering water until it thickens. Add sugar to taste. Meanwhile place a layer of raspberries and blackberries at the bottom of the ramekins, cover with cooled cream mixture. Place in fridge to set. Before serving sprinkle with crushed brandy snaps.

Meringue Pavlova filled with Strawberry or Raspberry Ice Cream Sprinkled with Raspberries

(Serves 6)

INGREDIENTS

For the Pavlova:

4 egg whites

8 oz (225g) caster sugar

4 teaspoons cornflour

2 teaspoons vinegar

½ teaspoon vanilla essence

METHOD

Beat egg whites, fold in sugar one spoon at a time, whisking until stiff. Fold in cornflour, vinegar and vanilla essence. Butter a shallow oven proof dish. Fill with mixture and hollow out the centre. Bake for 1¾ hours in slow oven 275°F/140°C/Gas 1. Cool. Will last for several weeks in a tin.

INGREDIENTS

For the Raspberry or Strawberry Ice Cream:

1 lb (450g) raspberries or strawberries

1 lb extra raspberries or strawberries for sprinkling

9 fl oz (250ml) double cream

1 tin Nestles condensed milk

METHOD

For the Raspberry or Strawberry Ice Cream:

Whizz raspberries or strawberries in liquidiser, sieve. Whip double cream, fold in sweetened condensed milk followed by sieved raspberries or strawberries. Freeze in container. When frozen, scoop into balls and lay on tray covered with baking paper and return to freezer. Take out 5 minutes before serving. Place in meringue pavlova. Decorate with sprinkled raspberries as photo.

Tip: Marvellous pudding for large numbers. It can be made days in advance and ice cream can be put in balls in deep freeze ready to use. To make balls take out of freezer, defrost for 10 minutes, have ready a mug of boiling water for dipping ice-cream baller into every time you scoop.

Elderflower Jelly with Mixed Fruit

(Serves 6)

INGREDIENTS
¼ pt (150ml) elderflower cordial
 (Add ½ pt cold water)
4 leaves gelatine (soaked in cold water)
1 punnet (150g) raspberries
1 punnet blueberries

METHOD
Heat cordial gently in small pan. Remove from heat, squeeze excess water from soaked gelatine leaves and add to cordial stirring till gelatine is dissolved. Pour into bowl and add ½ pint cold water (300ml) stir well. Divide jelly between 4 martini glasses when cold. Chill in fridge for about 1 hour until jelly has thickened. Add mixed fruit. Leave overnight. Serve with scoop of raspberry ice cream on top. (optional)

Wonderful when you have eaten a rather heavy dinner

Almost my favourite

Chocolate Bavarois

(Serves 4-6)

INGREDIENTS
4 oz (100g) sugar
1 pt (600ml) milk
4 egg yolks
3 oz (75g) dark chocolate (grated)
3 oz (75g) milk chocolate (grated)
½ pt (300ml) whipped cream
  and extra for decoration
3 sheets gelatine (place in cold water
  for few minutes, squeeze water
  out well and place in custard.
¼ pt (150ml) double cream
2 chocolate flakes

METHOD
Place sugar, milk, egg yolks and chocolate in pan and simmer stirring continuously (DO NOT BOIL) till thickens like custard. Cool. Then stir in gelatine and whipped cream. Pour into coffee cups and chill to set (4-6 hours). Sprinkle with chocolate flake.

Chocoholic!

My Mother's Recipe

Slides down too easily!

Chocolate Roulade Filled with Raspberries & Served with a Caramel Sauce

(Serves 6)

INGREDIENTS

5 egg yolks
5 egg whites (stiffly beaten)
3 tablespoons cocoa
  plus 2 tablespoons for dusting
4 oz (100g) icing sugar
1 pt (600ml) double cream
2 punnets (150g each) Raspberries

For the Caramel Sauce:

4 oz (100g) butter
6 oz (175g) soft brown sugar
½ pt (300ml) double cream

METHOD

Beat yolks until thick add sugar and beat again. Fold in cocoa powder well. Fold in stiffly beaten egg white. Pour on to baking tray 9"x12" (23cm x 30cm) lined with baking parchment. Bake at 350°F/180°C/Gas 4 for about 20 minutes. Cool, turn out onto baking parchment dusted with cocoa. Peel off parchment then spread with whipped cream. Sprinkle with raspberries, gently fold over with paper, slide carefully onto platter and dust with icing sugar. Decorate with Raspberries and serve with warm Caramel Sauce.

For the Caramel Sauce:

Place butter, sugar and cream in saucepan and heat gently till butter is melted and sugar dissolved. Simmer sauce for 3-5 minutes and serve warm with Roulade.

Coffee Crème with a Brandy Snap Crunch

(Serves 6)

INGREDIENTS

1 pt (600ml) whipping cream
2 teaspoons instant coffee granules
4 medium egg yolks
6 oz (150g) dulce de leche
caster sugar for glazing
brandy snaps

Oliver's Favourite

METHOD

Preheat the oven to 300°F/150°C/ Gas 2. Place the whipping cream and coffee in a pan and slowly bring to the boil. Meanwhile, mix the egg yolks and dulce de leche in large bowl. Remove the coffee cream from the heat, and whisk into the yolks. Pour into 6 ramekins or small coffee cups. Carefully place the dishes in a deep baking tray and pour hot water from the kettle to come two-thirds of the way up the sides of the dishes. Cover loosely with foil and bake for 40 minutes until just set, as the residual heat in the custard will continue the cooking process. Remove from the oven and water. Set aside to chill. Before serving crumble some brandy snap on top.

Orange Crème Caramel

(Serves 4)

INGREDIENTS

5 egg yolks plus 1 egg
6 oz (150g) caster sugar
1 orange and 1 grapefruit, in segments
¾ pt (450ml) double cream
½ pt (300ml) full-fat milk
4 teaspoons water
zest of 1 orange

METHOD

Mix together egg yolks, egg and half the sugar in bowl. Bring cream, milk and orange zest to boil in large pan. Remove from heat and cool for 10 minutes. Pour cream mixture over eggs and stir lightly with wooden spoon. Set aside. Melt rest of sugar in small pan over low heat till it begins to darken in colour. Remove from heat and stir in water very carefully to prevent sugar spitting and burning your skin. Pour into bottom of 4 ramekins. Cool. Fill with orange custard. Place in bain-marie (a roasting tin half filled with hot water) and bake at 300°F/150°C/Gas 2 for about 40 minutes till set. Cool. Chill in fridge for about 8 hours. To serve, slide knife around the edge and invert onto plate. Serve with orange and grapefruit segments.

Elderflower Panna Cotta Decorated with Raspberries & Blackberries

(Serves 4)

INGREDIENTS

¼ pt (150ml) whole milk
9 fl oz (250ml) double cream
1½ oz (40g) caster sugar
2 tablespoons elderflower cordial
2 gelatine leaves
1 teaspoon vanilla essence
1 punnet raspberries and/or blackberries
4 brandy snaps

METHOD

Mix milk, cream and sugar in saucepan, add vanilla essence and elderflower cordial. Set aside. Soak gelatine in bowl of cold water for 5 minutes till soft. Squeeze out excess water. Heat saucepan of ingredients, add gelatine. Stir well till dissolved. Leave to cool, pour mixture into ramekins. Chill over-night. Turn out panna cottas by dipping each ramekin very quickly into hot water. Serve with fruit and a brandy snap on the side.

Such a gentle smooth taste

Brandy Snaps or Lace Baskets

INGREDIENTS

2 oz (50g) butter
2 oz (50g) demerara sugar
3 tablespoons golden syrup
2 oz (50g) plain sifted flour

METHOD

Place butter, sugar and syrup in pan and heat gently till dissolved. Cool slightly then beat in flour. Place four heaped teaspoonfuls of mixture well apart onto baking sheets and bake at 350°F/180°C/ Gas 4 for 10-12 minutes till golden brown. Cool slightly (don't leave too long as they become too brittle to roll). Remove with palette knife and roll like a cigar or mould onto an orange to make a basket to serve fruit/ice cream etc. in.

I adore brandy snaps, they seem to have gone out of fashion nowadays but they are so delicious, so easy and so useful – and delicious as a crumbled topping.

Orange & Caramel Roulade

(Serves 8)

INGREDIENTS
For the Sponge:

3 large eggs
4 oz (100g) golden caster sugar
2 oz (50g) plain flour sifted
2 oz (50g) ground almonds
½ teaspoon baking powder
finely grated zest of 2 oranges
icing sugar

INGREDIENTS
For the Filling:

7 fl oz (200ml) double cream
4 oz (100g) white chocolate melted
bottle of M&S sticky toffee sauce
3 oranges peeled and segmented

METHOD

Whisk eggs and sugar till thick. Fold in flour, almonds, baking powder and zest of 2 oranges. Pour mixture onto Swiss roll tin (11¾" x 8") lined with baking parchment. Level it with a knife. Bake for 15 minutes at 350°F/180°C/Gas 4. Leave to cool for 10 minutes. Turn out onto new piece of parchment sprinkled with icing sugar. Whisk double cream until thick, add the melted chocolate, then whisk again. Spread onto roulade, drizzle with half of sticky toffee sauce. Roll up roulade with parchment. Drizzle with rest of sticky toffee sauce and decorate with orange segments. Serve with plain Orange Salad.

Oranges in Caramel Sauce

(Serves 4)

INGREDIENTS

8 oranges
4 oz (100g) caster sugar
¼ pt (150ml) water

METHOD

Peel oranges into large bowl and divide into segments by slicing down each segment to remove the pith. Put sugar in pan, melt carefully, no stirring. When completely melted add the water. Be careful as it will bubble up leave on low heat till all caramel has melted. Cool and pour over oranges. Serve with brandy snaps.

Caramel Cream

(Serves 4)

INGREDIENTS

1 pt (600ml) double cream
1 tin Nestles caramel sauce
1 punnet blackberries or raspberries
¼ pt (150ml) extra double cream

METHOD

Whip cream and add caramel. Place in coffee cups. Cool in fridge. To serve pour a little cream over top. Decorate with blackberries and place in fridge for 2 hours.

Orange and Lemon Creams

(Serves 4-6)

INGREDIENTS

1 pt (600ml) double cream
6 oz (150g) caster sugar
zest and juice of 2 lemons and 2 oranges
2 extra oranges for slices
1 sheet gelatine (placed in a little
    warm water for a few minutes
    and then squeezed out)

METHOD

Place the double cream and sugar in large saucepan (you will need a large saucepan as the mixture needs to boil vigorously). Add zest of oranges and lemons to cream. Bring the mixture to a rolling boil and allow it to boil vigorously for 5 minutes, whisking occasionally. Squeeze the juice from the lemons and oranges and add to the cream. Add gelatine and mix well. Remove from heat and strain through a sieve. Allow mixture to cool slightly and stir initially to prevent a skin from forming. Place 3 slices of orange at bottom of wine glass or ramekin. Divide mixture between glasses, cover and chill in fridge for a minimum of 4 hours, then allow to come back to room temperature for 10 minutes before serving. Place sliced oranges on top for decoration.

Tip: Delicious topped with raspberry coulis.

Norwegian Cream

(Serves 4)

INGREDIENTS

1 pt (600ml) full cream milk
½ pt (300ml) single cream
vanilla essence
2 whole eggs
5 egg yolks
1 tablespoons caster sugar
¼ pt (150ml) double cream
2-3 tablespoons apricot jam
grated Bournville chocolate
  for decoration

METHOD

Spoon apricot jam into bottom of soufflé dish. Heat milk and single cream in pan to boiling point. Beat eggs and egg yolks with caster sugar and add a few drops of vanilla essence. Mix a little of the hot milk/cream into egg mixture and then add the rest. Pour mixture on top of apricot jam. Place soufflé dish in bain-marie (a baking tin half filled with hot water) and bake at 325°F/170°C/Gas 3 for about 35 minutes till set. Cool. When chilled, cover with whipped double cream and sprinkle with chocolate.

Oliver at the Norwegian fjords

Oliver's
new hobby
silversmithing
in Banff

Kenny's Lemon Tart with Raspberry Ice Cream or Sorbet

(Serves 8)

INGREDIENTS

For the Sweet Pastry:

12 oz (350g) soft plain flour

6 oz (175g) butter

4 oz (100g) icing sugar

1 egg

For the Filling:

4 lemons (zest and juice)

9 large eggs

11 oz (300g) caster sugar

11 fl oz (325ml) double cream

For the Eggwash:

2 yolks

For the Dusting:

2 oz (50g) Icing sugar

METHOD

Start by making pastry, sift flour into bowl and rub in butter till it resembles fine breadcrumbs. Beat egg and add to centre of mixture. Bind together with a little water until you have a smooth dough. Refrigerate for 10 minutes. Roll sweet pastry to around 3mm thick and line a 10" x 1" (25cm x 2.5cm) deep flan tin. Cover the interior of the pastry case with baking parchment and fill with baking beans. Bake blind for approximately 25 minutes at 350°F/180°C/Gas 4. Remove baking beans and brush pastry with egg wash and return to the oven for 5 minutes until the pastry is glazed. In the meantime grate lemons and squeeze and strain juice and reserve. Beat eggs with sugar and lightly add lemon zest and juice. Lightly whisk in cream until smooth and blended. Lower oven temperature to 275°F/140°C/Gas 1. Pour the filling into the case. Bake for approximately 50-75 minutes depending on your oven or until the tart filling just wobbles and no more. Leave to cool for several hours, dust with icing sugar and serve.

The best in the world!

White Chocolate Lemon Curd Cheesecake with Chocolate Gingersnap Crust

(Serves 8)

INGREDIENTS

For the Gingersnap Crust:

7 oz (200g) ginger biscuits
  (blended into crumbs)
2 oz (50g) unsalted butter
1 tablespoon demerara sugar (optional)

For the Lemon Cheesecake Filling:

12 oz (350g) mascarpone cheese
4 oz (100g) caster sugar
finely grated rind of 1 large lemon
2 egg yolks
½ pint (300ml) cream
1 tablespoon limonchello liquer
  or Cointreau
2 egg whites
juice of 1 lemon
4 gelatine leaves
  (soaked in cold water to soften)

For the White Chocolate Lemon Curd topping:

1 egg
1 egg Yolk
2 oz (50g) caster sugar
zest of 1 lemon (peeled in large strips)
¼ cup lemon juice
3 oz (75g) white chocolate (chopped)

METHOD

Melt butter, mix in biscuit crumbs and demerara sugar. Press into individual rings or a 9" (23cm) loose bottomed cake tin. Mix cream cheese, sugar and lemon rind and beat until soft and creamy. Beat in salt, sugar and egg yolks. Whip liquer into the cream until it holds soft peaks. Whisk egg whites until stiff. Heat lemon juice and add softened gelatine and dissolve and stir into the cheese mixture. Fold in the whipped cream and beaten egg whites. Pour the mixture into prepared biscuit lined rings or tin. Chill while you make topping. For the white chocolate and lemon curd topping, whisk egg yolk in a medium bowl until blended. Stir in lemon juice and zest. Set bowl over a saucepan of barely simmering water. Cook stirring constantly with a wooden spoon for 5-6 minutes, or until mixture turns opaque and thickens and coats the back of the spoon. Strain mixture through a fine sieve and add chocolate, stirring until completely melted. Set aside to cool. Remove cheesecake from refrigerator and using a palette knife, spread over the topping. Return to the refrigerator for 1 hour to set topping. To serve decorate top of cheesecake with swirls of cream, berries and chocolate curls.

Tempting Teas

These recipes were given to me by our dear family friend Mrs Douglas who lived on the estate for over 50 years and was a superb cook

Mrs D's Quick Brown Bread with Sundried Tomatoes

INGREDIENTS

4 oz (100g) self-raising flour
8 oz (225g) wholemeal flour
  or granary flour
1 small teaspoon bicarbonate of soda
1 small teaspoon cream of tartar
1 small teaspoon sugar
½ pt (300ml) milk
4 oz (100g) sundried tomatoes
a pinch of salt

METHOD

Mix dry ingredients together. Add milk and mix well. Add sundried tomatoes. Pour into loaf tin, cover with foil and bake at 375F/190°C/Gas 5 for 35 minutes. Remove foil and bake for further 5 minutes.

Mrs D'S Quick White Bread

INGREDIENTS

4 oz (100g) self-raising flour
8 oz (225g) white flour
1 small teaspoon bicarbonate of soda
1 small teaspoon cream of tartar
1 small teaspoon sugar
½ pt (300ml) buttermilk
a pinch of salt

METHOD

Mix dry ingredients together. Add buttermilk and mix well. Pour into loaf tin, cover with foil and bake at 375°F/190°C/Gas 5 for 35 minutes. Remove foil and bake for further 5 minutes.

Ballindalloch Shortbread

INGREDIENTS

8 oz (225g) plain flour
4 oz (100g) cornflour
4 oz (100g) icing sugar
8 oz (225g) butter

METHOD

Chop butter into small pieces and place into processor with sieved flour, cornflour and icing sugar. Whizz until it gathers into a ball. Turn out onto floured surface and roll out to ½ inch thick. Cut into rounds with pastry cutter and place on greased baking tray. Cook for 15-20 mins at 350°F/180°C/Gas 4 till firm and light brown. Place on wire rack and sprinkle with caster sugar while warm.

TIP: To keep shortbread fresh and crisp place in plastic bag when cool, and then place in an airtight tin.

A must in every Scottish household

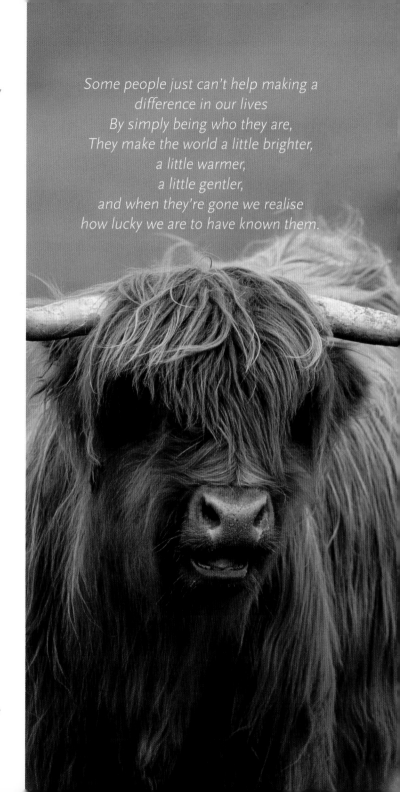

*Some people just can't help making a difference in our lives
By simply being who they are,
They make the world a little brighter,
a little warmer,
a little gentler,
and when they're gone we realise
how lucky we are to have known them.*

Lemon & Ginger Bread Sponge Tray Bake with Orange & Lemon Icing

INGREDIENTS

7 oz (200g) self raising flour
7 oz (200g) caster sugar
1 teaspoon ground ginger
2 teaspoons bicarbonate of soda
2 oz (50g) butter plus extra for greasing
1 free range egg beaten
2 tablespoons golden syrup
9 fl oz (225ml) hot water

For the Orange and Lemon Icing:

8 oz (225g) icing sugar
finely grated rind and juice of an orange
2 tablespoons lemon juice

METHOD

Preheat oven to 350°F/180°C/Gas 4. Grease a Swiss roll tin.
Mix flour, sugar, ginger and bicarbonate of soda together in bowl. Using your fingers rub the butter in until mixture resembles breadcrumbs. Add beaten egg, syrup and hot water and mix well with a wooden spoon until combined. Pour the mixture into prepared tin and bake in the middle of the oven for 35-40 minutes or until golden brown and the top is springy to the touch. Leave to cool in tin. Once cool add orange and lemon icing, then cut into squares.

For the Orange and Lemon Icing:

Mix lemon and orange juice and orange rind with sifted icing sugar in pan to the consistency of pouring cream. Heat till warm but not hot. Pour over ginger sponge, allow to cool and then cut into squares.

Truly yummy

White Chocolate & Toffee Shortbread

INGREDIENTS

2 oz (50g) butter
1 oz (25g) caster sugar
3 oz (75g) plain flour

For the Toffee:

4 oz (100g) butter
2 oz (50g) caster sugar
2 tablespoons golden syrup
½ x tin 7 oz (200g) sweetened
   condensed milk
few drops of vanilla essence

For the Topping:

8 oz (225g) white chocolate

METHOD

For the Base:

Rub flour, butter and sugar together until mixture resembles fine breadcrumbs. Press onto tin 8" x 12" (20cms x 30cms). Bake at 325°F/160°C/Gas 3 for about 20 minutes. Leave to cool.

For the Toffee and Topping:

Melt all toffee ingredients in pan and boil for 5 minutes stirring continually. Cool a little. Pour toffee over top. Cool. Melt chocolate in bowl over pan of boiling water and spread on top of toffee. When set cut into squares.

"Flap Jack" (Biggles Biscuits)

A twist on the old classic Flapjack with the addition of Fiery (Chocks away) Ginger, White Chocolate and Condensed Milk

INGREDIENTS

10 oz (275g) oats

5 oz (150g) unsalted butter

5 oz (150g) golden syrup (5 tbsp)

5 oz (150g) demerara sugar

7 oz (200g) condensed milk (½ 400g tin)

4 oz (100g) fiery crystallised ginger

4 oz (100g) packet white chocolate chips

1 oz (25g) extra white chocolate for
   decoration (optional)

oil/butter for greasing/ baking parchment
Oven 350°F/180°C/Gas 4

This recipe is very simple. For this
quantity of mix I use a 13½" x 4½" x 1"
deep tray bake tin which produces a nice
deep Flapjack. Brush tin with oil or butter
and line with baking parchment.

METHOD

Melt butter, sugar and syrup together.
Remove from heat, add condensed
milk, and crystallised ginger followed by
the oats. Press half of the mix into the
prepared baking tin then scatter over the
chocolate chips. Cover with the other half
of the mixture and press it level into the
tin ensuring there are no spaces. Bake
for 25-30 minutes or until golden brown.
These are lovely served warm, however
if you can resist, when completely cool
drizzle with a little white chocolate before
slicing into nice neat biscuits.

Illustrations by Sue Gordon

Apricot Whisky Fruit Cake

INGREDIENTS

6 oz (175g) demerara sugar

4 oz (100g) butter

1 tin (400g) apricots liquidised
   (without juice)

12 oz (350g) mixed fruit

4 oz (100g) cherries

1 tablespoon Glenfiddich whisky

2 eggs, beaten

9 oz (250g) self-raising flour

METHOD

Simmer first 5 ingredients in pan for a few minutes. Add 2 beaten eggs and 9 oz (250g) self-raising flour. Add cherries. Mix in whisky. Bake in 2lb bread tin for 1¼-1½ hours at 350°F/180°C/Gas 4.

Deliciously moist, keeps well and is ideal to leave in a tin for the unexpected visitor

St Clement's Traybake

INGREDIENTS

7 oz (200g) plain flour
2 teaspoons baking powder
7 oz (200g) caster sugar
4 eggs
¼ pt (150ml) soured cream
grated rind of 1 large lemon
4 tablespoons lemon juice
¼ pt (150ml) sunflower oil

For the syrup:
4 tablespoons icing sugar
3 tablespoons lemon juice

For the icing:
8 oz (225g) fondant icing sugar
finely grated rind and juice of ½ orange
2 tablespoons lemon juice

90 plus birthday party in Banffshire
to celebrate the Queen's 90th Birthday.

METHOD

Grease and line a baking tin 8½" x 12" (22cm x 30cm). Sieve flour and baking powder and mix in sugar. Whisk (or blend in food processor) eggs, soured cream, lemon rind and juice and oil. Add dry ingredients and mix well. Pour mixture into the prepared tin and bake in pre-heated oven 350°F/180°C/Gas 4 for about 25-30 minutes until risen and golden.

To make syrup, stir lemon juice and icing sugar in pan over low heat until just beginning to bubble and turn syrupy. Brush the syrup over the top of the sponge as soon as it comes out of the oven.

To make the icing, mix the lemon and orange juices and orange rind with the sifted fondant icing sugar in pan to the consistency of pouring cream. Warm through on low heat to a temperature which would feel uncomfortably hot to the hand. Pour immediately over the soaked sponge and allow to set. Make up a little extra icing, add colour, and pipe lines across traybake. Leave the traybake to cool completely in the tin. When set, cut into squares.

Empire Biscuits

INGREDIENTS

4 oz (100g) butter (soft)

4 oz (100g) caster sugar

1 egg

10 oz (275g) flour

4 teaspoons raspberry/strawberry jam

4 oz (100g) icing sugar

6 glace cherries (halved)

METHOD

Beat butter and caster sugar till pale and creamy. Add egg and beat again before adding the flour. Mix to form dough. Wrap dough in cling film for 30 minutes. Line 2 baking sheets with baking parchment. Roll out the chilled dough onto dusted work top to 2-3cm depth. Cut into 7cm rounds and place on prepared baking sheets. Put in oven and bake at 375°F/190°C/Gas 5 for 10-12 minutes until light golden. Cool for few minutes. Sandwich together with jam. Make icing by mixing two teaspoons of boiled water with icing sugar till smooth. Then spread evenly over tops of rounds. Top with half cherry and leave to cool.

Mrs D's Mouth Watering Gingerbread & Date Cake

INGREDIENTS

8 oz (225g) plain flour

4 oz (100g) margarine

6 fl oz (175ml) black treacle

2 oz (50g) golden syrup

2 oz (50g) granulated sugar

¼ pt (150ml) milk

1 teaspoon baking soda

1 teaspoon ground ginger

2 eggs beaten

1 packet chopped dates

METHOD

Melt margarine syrup and treacle in pan. Add ¼ pt (150ml) milk. Cool. Add beaten eggs. Mix dry ingredients together and add to pan. Mix well and fold in stoned, chopped dates. Line loaf tin with non-stick baking paper and bake at 325°F/160°C/Gas 3 for 1¼ -1½ hours.

A never-fail recipe which always turns out superbly moist and keeps well

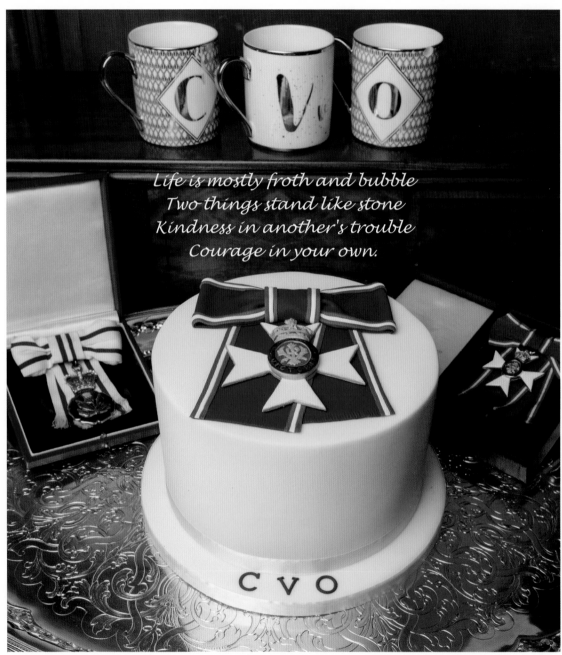

Life is mostly froth and bubble
Two things stand like stone
Kindness in another's trouble
Courage in your own.

Jo Robinson

Elizabeth R

Elizabeth the Second, by the Grace of God of the
United Kingdom of Great Britain and Northern Ireland and of Her
other Realms and Territories Queen, Head of the Commonwealth,
Defender of the Faith and Sovereign of the Royal Victorian Order to Our
trusty and well beloved *Clare Nancy Russell Our Lord-Lieutenant of
Banffshire*

Greeting

Whereas We have thought fit to nominate and appoint you to be
a Commander of Our said Royal Victorian Order

We do by these presents grant unto you the Dignity of a
Commander of Our said Order and hereby authorise you to have hold and
enjoy the said Dignity and Rank of a Commander of Our aforesaid
Order together with all and singular the privileges thereunto belonging or
appertaining.

Given at Our Court at Saint James's under Our Sign Manual
and the Seal of Our said Order this Seventeenth day of June 2017 in the
Sixty-sixth year of Our Reign.

By the Sovereign's Command.

Anne

Grand Master.

Grant of the Dignity of a Commander
of the Royal Victorian Order
to *Clare Nancy, Mrs. Russell*

Chancellor.

Kenny's Chocolate Hearts

INGREDIENTS

For the Base:

2 oz (50g) melted butter

1 oz (25g) grape-nuts cereal

7 oz (200g) chocolate coated
  ginger biscuits

For the Filling:

5½ oz (160g) dark chocolate (melted)

9 oz (250g) tub ricotta cheese

4 oz (100g) cream cheese eg. mascarpone

7 oz (200g) crème fraîche

2 eggs (separated)

3 leaves gelatine
  (soaked in cold water to soften)

2 tbs hot water

For the Chocolate Mirror Glaze:

3 leaves gelatine
  (soaked in cold water to soften)

6 oz (170g) granulated sugar

100ml water

4½ oz (115g) dark chocolate

¾ oz (20g) coca powder

65ml cream

*If you don't want to make
your own mirror glaze,
it is widely available now
on supermarket shelves.*

METHOD

For the Base:

Crush biscuits and add to bowl with grape-nuts cereal. Bind together with melted butter and press into heart rings.

For the Filling:

Whisk together, ricotta, cream cheese, crème fraîche, egg yolks and sugar until smooth and blended. Squeeze excess water from gelatine and add to 2 tbs hot water to dissolve. Stir into ricotta mixture until it is thoroughly blended. Whisk egg whites to soft peaks and gently incorporate into ricotta mixture. Pour mixture onto the biscuit bases and chill in the fridge for a few hours. Un-mould and transfer to a baking wire.

For the Chocolate Mirror Glaze:

Boil water and sugar to 104°C. Add chocolate and blend then mix in cocoa powder, followed by the cream. When the mixture is around 60°C add gelatine. Mix with a hand blender and pour through a fine sieve. Work mix at around 33°C and pour over hearts. Garnish with some melted white chocolate.

Golden Wedding
1967–2017

When You Are Lonely

When you are lonely, I wish you love
When you are down, I wish you joy
When you are troubled, I wish you simply beauty
When things are chaotic, I wish you inner silence
When things look empty, I wish you hope
I wish for both of you, a giant book imprinted on your souls
Where you shall keep all the memories you will make together
I wish for a group of angels hovering over both of you
Every second, every minute of your lives
I wish for both of you, happiness and the faith to see
That God blessed you both then He gave you to each other

Anonymous

Clare & Oliver

happily married since

16 | 09 | 1967

fifty fabulous years

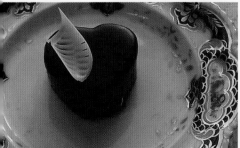

Orange Scones & Castle Marmalade

INGREDIENTS

8 oz (225g) sieved self-raising flour
1½ teaspoons baking powder
1 oz (25g) soft brown sugar
pinch of salt
2 oz (50g) butter
grated zest of 1 orange
5 oz (125ml) plain yoghurt

For the Castle Marmalade:

3 lb Seville oranges
2 lemons
6 pints of water
3 lb preserving sugar
3 lb jam sugar

METHOD

Mix flour, sugar and salt with baking powder and rub in butter. Add orange zest and yoghurt. Mix to a dough. Knead briefly and pat out to 1" (2.5cm) thick. Cut into rounds with pastry cutter. Place rounds on greased and floured baking tray and bake at 400°F/200°C/Gas 6 for 10-12 minutes till risen and golden.

For the Castle Marmalade:

Wash and dry the Oranges. Peel the zest and slice into fine strips and add to a large pan. Halve the oranges and juice – reserving the pips. Sieve juice into the pan with the juice from the lemons. Scoop away the remaining fruit from the pith. Chop and add to the pan. Chop the pith and tie into a muslin cloth with the reserved pips. Add to the pan with 6 pints of water. Bring to the boil and simmer for 2½ hours until the zest tender and the liquid has reduced by half. Remove and squeeze the muslin bag to extract as much pectin juice back into the pan. Discard the remaining contents of the muslin. Now add the sugar to the pan and bring to a rolling boil for around 20 minutes or until the setting point has been achieved. Allow to settle for ½ hour then pour into sterilised jars.

A great treat for
breakfast served with
Kenny's home-made
Castle marmalade

Caramel Empire Biscuits

INGREDIENTS

8 oz (225g) plain flour
4 oz (100g) cornflour
4 oz (100g) icing sugar
8 oz (225g) butter

For the Toffee:

4 oz (100g) butter
2 oz (50g) caster sugar
2 tablespoons golden syrup
½ tin (7 oz/200g) sweetened
  condensed milk

METHOD

Chop butter into small pieces and place in processor with sieved flour, cornflour and icing sugar. Whizz until it gathers into a ball. Turn out onto floured surface and roll out to ½ inch thick. Cut into rounds with pastry cutter and place on greased baking tray. Cook for 15-20 minutes at 350°F/180°C/Gas 4 till firm and light brown. Place on wire rack and cool.

For the Toffee:

Melt all toffee ingredients in pan and boil for 5 minutes stirring continually. Cool a little and sandwich between 2 shortbreads. Spread a little on top of shortbread and decorate with a little grated chocolate.

Francesca's Chocolate Chip Cookies

(Makes 30 cookies)

INGREDIENTS

7 oz (200g) salted butter (softened)

3 oz (75g) granulated sugar

3 oz (75g) light brown muscovado sugar

2 teaspoons Vanilla extract

1 large egg

8 oz (225g) plain flour

½ teaspoon bicarbonate of soda

¼ teaspoon salt

7 oz (200g) plain chocolate chips
  or chunks

METHOD

Heat the oven to 375°F/190°C/Gas 5 and line two baking sheets with non-stick baking paper.

Put softened salted butter, light brown muscovado sugar and granulated sugar into a bowl and beat until creamy. Beat in 2 teaspoons vanilla extract and 1 large egg. Sift flour and bicarbonate of soda and salt into the bowl and mix with wooden spoon. Add plain chocolate chips or chunks and stir well.

Use a teaspoon to make small scoops of the mixture, spacing them well apart on the baking trays.

Bake for 8-10 minutes until they are light brown on the edges and still slightly soft in the centre if you press them. Leave on the tray for a couple of minutes to set and then lift onto a cooking rack.

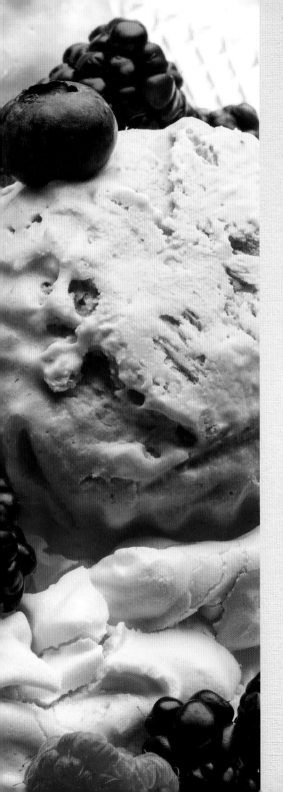

Interesting Ice Creams

Wonderful to have in the deep freeze
when you have unexpected visitors

Clotted Cream, Honey & Whisky Ice Cream

(Serves 4-6)

INGREDIENTS
1 jar (150ml) clotted cream
½ pt (300ml) double cream
1 tin condensed milk
2½ fl oz (60ml) whisky
2½ fl oz (60ml) honey

METHOD
Mix clotted cream and double cream together. Add condensed milk then whisky and honey. Place in deep freeze. Take out 15–20 minutes before serving.

Strawberry or Raspberry Ice Cream

(Serves 4)

INGREDIENTS
1¾ lbs (750g) strawberries
juice of 2 lemons
1 pt (600ml) double cream
1 tin Nestles condensed milk

METHOD
Hull strawberries. Whizz to purée. Stir in lemon juice. Whip double cream to soft peaks. Fold in sweetened condensed milk followed by strawberry purée. Freeze in container. Take out 20 minutes before serving.

Delicious served in meringue nests or brandy snap baskets sprinkled with a few raspberries.

So easy to take out of the deep freeze when time is not a word in your vocabulary!

Salted Caramel Ice Cream with Chopped Tablet

(Serves 6)

INGREDIENTS

1 pt (600ml) double cream
tin (397g) of caramel or dulce de leche
pinch salt (to taste)
raspberries to decorate
10 fudge tablets or packet of
  Cotswold fudge

METHOD

Whip double cream till holding its shape. Add caramel and a pinch of salt. Fold in chopped fudge. Place in freezer proof container and freeze for 6-8 hours. Take out 15 minutes before serving. Accompany with raspberries, or delicious with young rhubarb.

DIVINE - I must NOT make it again!!

After Eight Mint Ice Cream

(Serves 4)

INGREDIENTS

1 oz (25g) caster sugar
4 fl oz (110ml) water
½ lb (225g) box of After Eight Mints
3 egg yolks (beaten)
¼ pt (150ml) double cream
brandy to taste
6 chocolate cups

METHOD

Heat sugar in water slowly to melt. Then boil fast for 3 minutes. Whizz 6 oz (175g) of mints in processor with egg yolks then add hot syrup. Cool a little, add cream and brandy to taste. Pour into chocolate cups, cover with cling film and freeze. Serve straight from freezer and decorate with After Eight mints cut in half.

Lemon Ice Cream

(Serves 6)

INGREDIENTS
6 egg yolks
8 oz (225g) caster sugar
2 lemons (grated rind and juice)
½ pt (300ml) double cream

METHOD
Beat egg yolks with sugar till thick and creamy. Fold in grated rind and juice of lemons. Whip cream and fold into mixture. Freeze. Remove from freezer 10-15 minutes before serving. Decorate with lemon slices and serve with shortbread.

P.S. Delicious served with a raspberry coulis

Served with a raspberry coulis

2 lb (1kg) raspberries
4 oz (100g) caster sugar

Liquidise and sieve.

Truly addictive

Lemon Sorbet

(Serves 4)

INGREDIENTS
7 oz (200g) caster sugar
4 lemons (well washed)
1 egg white

METHOD
Place sugar in pan and pour in ½ pt (300ml) water. Bring to boil stirring occasionally till sugar has dissolved. Using vegetable peeler, pare 2 lemons into pan and simmer for 2 minutes. Leave to cool. Squeeze juice from all lemons and add it to syrup. Strain syrup into container and freeze the mixture for about four hours until it is mushy. Then whizz sorbet in processor till smooth. Lightly whisk egg white with fork till frothy. Replace sorbet in container beat in egg white and put in freezer for at least 4 hours. Serve in glass dish with a brandy snap on the side.

Perfect after a heavy dinner

Pineapple Bomb Alaska

(Serves 4)

INGREDIENTS
1 pineapple (or 1 baby pineapple each)
3 egg whites
6 oz (150g) caster sugar

For the Ice Cream Mixture:
1 pt (600ml) double cream
1 large tin Nestles condensed milk
6 broken meringues

METHOD
Whisk cream and condensed milk till thick. Add crumbled meringue and place in freezer. Cut pineapple in half lengthways and scoop out pulp. When ice cream is frozen scoop it into the two halves of the pineapple and cover with some of the pulp. Whisk egg whites, fold in caster sugar and spread over pineapple. Bake in hot oven 425°F/220°C/ Gas 7 for about 3 minutes until meringue is golden. Serve immediately.

Mango Ice Cream

(Serves 4)

INGREDIENTS
15 oz (425g) tin
   mango purée or
   sliced mangos
   (liquidised)
1 pt (600ml) double cream
1 tin Nestles condensed milk

METHOD
Whip double cream to soft peaks, fold in remaining ingredients and freeze.

Wonderfully easy and quick

A most magic, unusual pudding –
It looks sensational and is incredibly easy to make.

Meringue Ice Cream Terrine with Raspberries

I have no will power! Delicious

(Serves 4-6)

INGREDIENTS
1 pt (600ml) double cream
1 tin Nestles condensed milk
6 large meringues

For the Topping:
8 oz (225g) raspberries
  + a few extra for decoration
raspberry coulis

For the Raspberry Coulis:
8 oz (225g) raspberries
1-2 tablespoons icing sugar

METHOD
Whip double cream till stiff. Add condensed milk and fold in well. Add crumbled meringues. Mix in thoroughly. Line a 3" (7cm) deep 9" x 4" (22cm x 10cm) loaf tin with a double layer of cling film so it hangs over edge. Pour mixture in and freeze. To serve take out 15 minutes before serving. To decorate place raspberries on top of terrine and then dribble all over the raspberry coulis. It may be easier to slice terrine and place each slice on desert plate and decorate with raspberries and dribble with coulis. That does look pretty. Can be put in freezer on tray lined with parchment and taken out and served straight away.

For the Raspberry Coulis:
Liquidise all and sieve

Peanut Butter Ice Cream

(Serves 4-6)

INGREDIENTS

1 tin condensed milk
½ jar crunchy peanut butter
½ jar smooth peanut butter
1 pt (600ml) double cream

METHOD

Whip double cream and then fold in condensed milk. Add peanut butter and mix in well. Freeze overnight. Take out the freezer 15 minutes before serving.

Raspberry and Rose Sorbet

(Serves 4)

INGREDIENTS

11 oz (300g) caster sugar
½ tablespoon rose water
1 lb (500g) raspberries
½ (300ml) water

METHOD

Place water in pan with caster sugar over low heat and stir till sugar dissolves, then bring to boil and boil rapidly for 3 minutes to give a light syrup. Remove pan from heat and leave syrup to cool. Stir in rose water! Liquidise raspberries and sieve. Stir purée into cooled syrup. Pour into container, freeze, beating regularly so it has a smooth texture or churn mixture in an ice cream machine.

Delightful

The White Rose of Scotland

The rose of all the world is not for me.
I want for my part
Only the little white rose of Scotland
That smells sharp and sweet – and breaks the heart.

Hugh MacDiarmid, 1934.
The Little White Rose.

Copper Dog

Whisky Galore

Have a dram at Ballindalloch Distillery

BALLINDALLOCH SINGLE MALT SCOTCH WHISKY

Ballindalloch Haggis Mousselines with a Whisky Cream & Onion Sauce

(Serves 4-6)

INGREDIENTS

8 oz (225g) haggis
6 oz (150g) turnip
6 oz (150g) creamed potatoes
seasoning
finely chopped parsley and
  chives for decoration

For the Sauce:

1 finely sliced onion
1 generous glass Ballindalloch whisky
½ pt (300ml) double cream

For the Chef:

1 small glass whisky

METHOD

Cook turnip and mash with a little butter and seasoning. Cook potatoes and mash well (no lumps) with a little butter and seasoning. Cook haggis by wrapping in foil and placing in oven 350°F/180°C/Gas 4 for about 45 minutes. Assemble mousselines by layering turnip, haggis and lastly creamed potato into buttered ramekins. Place ramekins in bain-marie (roasting tin half filled with boiling water) and bake at 350°F/180°C/Gas 4 for about 20-25 minutes. Meanwhile, make whisky sauce. Heat whisky in pan, take off heat and ignite. Pour in double cream and finely chopped onion and heat till boiling point. Keep warm. To serve, take ramekins out of oven, run knife round edge of them and invert onto plate. Drizzle with whisky sauce and sprinkle with finely chopped parsley and chives.

"In Heaven itself, I'll ask no more, than just a Highland welcome"

Robert Burns

Ballindalloch Beef Tournedos with a Whisky Cream Sauce

(Serves 6)

INGREDIENTS

2 Aberdeen Angus fillet steaks
   about 1" (2.5cm) thick
2 rounds of fried bread
2 oz (50g) butter
1 finely chopped onion
4 oz (100g) sliced mushrooms
¼ pt (150ml) cream
1 tablespoon whisky
2 teaspoons chopped parsley
2 oz (50g) pâté

METHOD

Melt butter in pan and cook steaks until done as desired. Remove from pan and keep warm. Fry onion and mushrooms in pan with butter. Add whisky, cream, chopped parsley and seasoning. Simmer for few minutes. Spread fried bread round with pâté. Place beef on round and serve whisky sauce separately.

A Scottish Touch to Chicken Liver Pâté

(Serves 4-6)

INGREDIENTS

4 oz (100g) butter
1 finely chopped onion
8 oz (225g) chicken livers
8 oz (225g) cream cheese
seasoning
1 tablespoon whisky (to taste)
4 rashers grilled streaky bacon
1 packet oatcakes
cranberry sauce

METHOD

Melt butter and fry onion till transparent. Add chicken livers (cut away any veins) and fry till just pink in the middle. Place in liquidiser with cream cheese and process. Add seasoning and whisky to taste. Place in pâté dish and fold in finely chopped grilled bacon. Cool. Melt some butter and pour over top of pâté. Chill and serve with oatcake and cranberry sauce.

Highland Bread & Butter Pudding with Apricot Glaze

(Serves 6-8)

INGREDIENTS

12 slices brioche bread

2 oz (50g) softened butter

3 oz (75g) raisins

3 oz (75g) sultans

3 tablespoons whisky (to taste)

1 oz (25g) heather honey

7 egg yolks and 1 whole egg

5 oz (125g) caster sugar

½ pt (300ml) milk

½ pt (300ml) double cream

2 teaspoons vanilla essence

2 tablespoons demerara sugar

icing sugar for dusting

For the Apricot Glaze:

4 oz (100g) apricot jam boiled with 2 fl oz (60ml) water to make a hot sticky glaze.

METHOD

Grease a 3 pint pudding dish with butter. Soak the raisins and sultanas in the whisky for 4 hours. Spread each slice of bread with the softened butter and a mere scraping of heather honey. Remove the crusts and cut in half diagonally twice, creating 4 triangles per slice. Arrange the bread in layers in the prepared ovenproof dish, scattering the raisins and sultanas between the layers.

Whisk the egg yolks, extra egg and caster sugar together. Bring the milk and cream to simmer. Pour the hot cream mixture over the egg yolks and sugar mixture. Add the vanilla essence. You now have a custard. Pour the custard over the bread and sprinkle with demerara sugar. Bake in a bain-marie (a baking tin half-filled with hot water) in a pre-heated oven at 350°F/180°C/Gas 4 for 20-30 minutes until the pudding begins to set. When ready, remove from the water bath. Dust with some icing sugar and glaze under the grill on medium heat.

Make the apricot glaze by boiling the apricot jam and water together. Brush on coating of glaze over the pudding. It is now ready to serve.

A Short History Of Ballindalloch Distillery

My family has lived at Ballindalloch since 1546. We are one of the very few castles in Scotland that has been lived in continuously by the same family for over 500 years.

Following in the footsteps of Sir George we decided in 2014 to build a small distillery in one of our steadings.

So much of what we do on the Estate has a historical nature and we wanted to reflect that in the Distillery. So much of the modern whisky industry requires automation and production on a massive scale. To that end, we decided to try to embrace an attitude that my ancestor would be familiar with. Our seven springs provide the glorious water from the hill behind, we grow all of our own barley, feed the left over draff to the Aberdeen Angus herd, fertilise our own fields with any residual liquids and the Distillery itself is fully manually operated. In a world of touch screens and e-mail, we are a quill pen and parchment.

All of our hard work was celebrated at the official opening in April 2015 when we had the pleasure of hosting TRH The Duke and Duchess of Rothesay during their visit to the Distillery. Wherever possible, we use the most locally based trades and craftsmen in all aspects of the project and to be able to invite them to a Royal opening was particularly rewarding. Our aims for the Distillery are for it to produce a light, fruity, sweet and complex spirit that the Speyside region is renowned for. One that my ancestors would recognise and one that we as a family together with the Distillery staff are proud to call Ballindalloch Single Malt Scotch Whisky. It is with great excitement that we look forward to the first anticipated bottling in 2023. Having already won two icons of Whisky awards for Craft Producer of the Year, we have high hopes for what is to come.

"Too much of anything is bad, but too much good whiskey is barely enough."

Mark Twain

Heather Honey &
Whisky Cheesecake with Raspberries

(Serves 2)

INGREDIENTS
4 ginger biscuits
5 oz (150g) full fat soft cheese
2 fl oz (50ml) double cream
1 tablespoon caster sugar
2 tablespoons runny heather
   or blossom honey
whisky to taste
5 oz (125g) punnet of raspberries

METHOD
Place 2 x 3½" (9cm) rings on 2 small
dessert plates. Liquidise ginger biscuits
until like fine breadcrumbs and divide
between the rings, kneading into the rings
to make a base. Place soft cheese in bowl
and whisk together with double cream,
sugar, two tablespoons of runny honey
and two tablespoons whisky, until thick.
Spoon mixture into rings, then spread
the top flat. Chill until ready to serve and
place raspberries on top.

Chocolate Truffles with Whisky

(Makes about 12)

INGREDIENTS
8 oz (200g) Bournville chocolate
4 oz (100g) unsalted butter
few drops of whisky
cocoa
grated chocolate

METHOD
Break chocolate into pyrex bowl and melt over pan of simmering water. Take bowl off heat and beat in butter gradually. Add whisky to taste. Refrigerate for several hours. Scoop out teaspoonfuls of mixture and shape in cocoa floured hands. Roll in cocoa or grated chocolate.

Alternative Recipe:

INGREDIENTS
8 oz (200g) Bournville chocolate
½ pt (300ml) double cream
grated chocolate, cocoa or chopped nuts

METHOD
Melt chocolate over pan of simmering water. Cool. Fold whipped cream into melted, cooled chocolate. Place in fridge till firm then shape into little balls and roll in grated chocolate, nuts or cocoa.

Oranges Drizzled in Whisky Sauce

(Serves 4)

INGREDIENTS
8 oranges
2 oz (25g) caster sugar
whisky to taste

METHOD
Peel oranges into large bowl and divide into segments by slicing down each segment to remove the pith. Add sugar and drizzle whisky (to taste) over top. Serve with Ballindalloch shortbread.

Wonderful Scottish Tablet (Fudge)

INGREDIENTS
1½ lb (675g) granulated sugar
3 oz (75g) butter
2 small tins of carnation milk
1-2 tablespoons whisky

METHOD
Bring sugar, whisky, milk and butter slowly to the boil, stirring occasionally. Boil for 25-30 minutes. Take off heat and beat till thick. Pour into greased tin, leave to cool for ½ hour. Cut into squares in tin and leave to cool for another 2 hours.

Clotted Cream, Honey & Whisky Ice Cream

(Serves 4-6)

INGREDIENTS

1 jar (150ml) clotted cream
½ pt (300ml) double cream
1 tin condensed milk
2½ fl oz (60ml) whisky
2½ fl oz (60ml) honey

METHOD

Mix clotted cream and double cream together. Add condensed milk then whisky and honey. Place in deep freeze. Take out 15–20 minutes before serving.

Going nuts for Norfolks

Doggie Master Chef

Woof
Dotty About Dogs

More Recipes for our Best Friends

Dogs are another of my great passions. I had no brothers or sisters, but my first beloved black Pekinese filled the gap. Ever since, I have been 'dotty about dogs'. They are the love of my life; they think you are wonderful, they love you to bits, they are totally loyal, they are your best friend, they don't argue, they don't answer back, and they greet you as a long lost friend when you come in. They are wonderful companions and always make you happy, even when they have just rolled in a dead salmon or deer! They are also wonderful visitors for people in care homes and those with special needs, who are unable to have a dog of their own.

Cheddar Cheese & Bacon Treats

I could eat these happily!

INGREDIENTS
1½ cups rolled oats
½ cup grated cheese
4 strips streaky bacon
2 eggs

METHOD
Place oats, cheese and streaky bacon into liquidiser and process till crumb-like. Add 2 eggs and process till sticky dough. Sprinkle flour on board and roll out dough till ¼" thick. Using a cookie cutter, cut out dough into bone shapes. Place on baking tray lined with baking parchment and cook for 20 minutes at 350°F/180°C/Gas 4. Cool and place in tin.

It's an exhausting world!

Spoiled Dog Cake

Wonderful birthday cake

INGREDIENTS
1 cup flour
½ teaspoon baking powder
⅛ cup vegetable oil
¼ cup peanut butter (xylitol free)
½ cup apple sauce
1 egg
doggie chocolate drops for decoration

METHOD
Combine flour and baking powder in bowl. In another bowl mix together vegetable oil, peanut butter and apple sauce. Mix well and then add egg. Mix in dry ingredients. Pour mixture into greased 8" (20cm) baking tin. Bake at 350°F/180°C/Gas 4 for 25-30 minutes. Cool on wire rack. Decorate with thin layer of melted doggie chocolate buttons.

Doggie Chocolate Crunch

To be eaten in small amounts - not gobbled!

INGREDIENTS

1½ cups porridge oats
2 eggs
1 packet doggie chocolates

METHOD

Place oats in liquidiser and process till crumb like. Add 2 eggs and process till sticky dough. Roll out on floured board and cut into shapes. Place on baking tray lined with parchment and cook for 20 minutes at 350°F/180°C/
Gas 4 for 20 minutes. When cool, spread melted chocolate over top. Cut into squares when set.

My Doggie Master Chef.

Peanut Butter Cookie Bones

Hip, hip Hooray Peanut butter!

INGREDIENTS

½ cup peanut butter (xylitol free)
2 eggs
¼ cup oil
2½ cups whole wheat flour
1 teaspoon baking powder

METHOD

Place peanut butter, eggs and oil in bowl. Add whole wheat flour and baking soda. Mix well and stir till stiff dough. Knead until all flour is mixed in well. Roll out dough and cut into shape and place on baking tray lined with baking parchment and bake at 350°F/180°C/Gas 4 for 15-20 minutes. Cool and place in tin.

Josie & Thomas's Special Treats – a Doggy Bribe!

I couldn't resist putting this in again – it's still the favourite.

METHOD

Take a pound of liver (any kind) and an egg. Liquidise in a blender or food processor and add enough flour to make a stiff, scone-like mixture. Spread out in a Swiss roll tin and bake at 350°F/180°C/Gas 4 for about 20 minutes in a fan, or 30 minutes in a regular oven. Ends up looking like rather solid chocolate cake. Cut into strips and freeze, taking out when needed.

Unfortunately, in the making of it the smell is somewhat overpowering and lingering, so we suggest you make it outside!

By John Laine

A Doddle for Dogs

Yum Yum

INGREDIENTS

2 cups of flour
½ cup peanut butter (xylitol free)
2 eggs

METHOD

Mix well all ingredients together, then add water till it is wet enough to roll out dough onto a parchment lined baking tray and then bake at 350°F/180°C/Gas 4 for 15-20 minutes. Cool and store in tin.

All mine!

It's a Dog's Life!

Weights & Measures
- but the scales always lie!

OVEN TEMPERATURE CHART

°C	°F	Gas Mark
110	225	¼
130	250	½
140	275	1
150	300	2
170	325	3
180	350	4
190	375	5
200	400	6
220	425	7
230	450	8
240	475	9

SPOON MEASUREMENTS

1 teaspoon	5 mls
4 teaspoons approximately	1 tablespoon
1 tablespoon approximately	20 mls
1 rounded spoon	2 level spoons

METRIC CONVERSION SCALE

LIQUID			SOLID		
Imperial	Exact Conversion	Recommended ml	Imperial	Exact Conversion	Recommended g
¼ pint	142 ml	150 ml	1 oz	28.35 g	25 g
½ pint	284 ml	300 ml	2 oz	56.7 g	50 g
1 pint	568 ml	600 ml	4 oz	113.4 g	100 g
1½ pints	851 ml	900 ml	8 oz	226.8 g	225 g
1¾ pints	992 ml	1 litre	12 oz	340.2 g	350 g
			14 oz	397.0 g	400 g
			16 oz (1 lb)	453.6 g	450 g
			2.2 lb	1 kilogram (kg)	

Leaf gelatine

soak in ice cold water

until softened

squeeze out & dissolve into hot liquid

AMERICAN CONVERSION OF WEIGHTS AND MEASURES
(Note: UK ounces and metric grams are weighed)

	US Standard	UK	Metric
Flour	¼ cup	1 oz	25 g
	½ cup	2 oz	50 g
	¾ cup	3 oz	75 g
	1 cup	4 oz	100 g
Icing Sugar/Cocoa/Cornflour	1 cup	4½ oz	120 g
Butter/Sugar	2 tbsp	1 oz	25 g
(caster, granulated or brown, firmly packed)	¼ cup	2 oz	50 g
	½ cup	4 oz	100 g
	¾ cup	6 oz	175 g
	1 cup	8 oz	225 g
Liquids/Cream/Yogurt	¼ cup	2.5 fl oz	60 ml
	½ cup	5 fl oz	120 ml
	¾ cup	7.5 fl oz	180 ml
	1 cup	10 fl oz	240 ml
	1 pt (2 cups)	20 fl oz	480 ml
Grated Cheese/Chopped Nuts	1 cup	4 oz	100 g
Yeast	1 cake, pkg	4 oz fresh	15 g
Rice	1 cup	8 oz	230 g

FOOD LEVEL

	spoons to 1 oz (25 g) (approximate equivalents)
Flour, cornflour and other starch powders	2 tablespoons
Fresh breadcrumbs and cake crumbs	4 tablespoons
Rolled oats	3 tablespoons
Rice	2 tablespoons
Sugar	2 tablespoons
Sultanas, seedless raisins, currants	2 tablespoons
Butter	2 tablespoons
Gelatine	3 tablespoons
Syrup, treacle, honey	1 tablespoon

Index

This "Third Helping" of I Love Food would never have come about without the wonderful skills and enthusiasm of Diana Campbell and Kenny Flesh – of course not forgetting my wonderful 'Chief Taster' Oliver and my four greedy dogs!

Also an enormous thank you goes to Guy, Edward and Lucy; to John Paul, Andrea De Pree and Tricia Lawson who yet again have produced the most fabulous photos; and to Jo Robinson who made the CVO cake. Jamieson Eley from Jarrolds has been a star and so helpful in putting the book together – not forgetting Sue Durrant and Fenella Corr for all their typing and advice.

I do hope you will enjoy 'I Love Food 3' as much as my other books, I have adored putting it together.

I have happiness four times a day!
Breakfast, Lunch, Tea and Dinner.

Happy Cooking

Clare Macpherson-Grant Russell

Clare Russell

Many apologies to anyone I have omitted; I have made every effort to contact all contributors, and copyright holders of images and written content. If any omissions have occurred, I apologise, and amendments will be incorporated in any subsequent editions.

Designed by Jamieson Eley

JARROLD
publishing

Published by Jarrold Publishing
Email: publications@jarrold-publishing.co.uk
www.jarrold-publishing.co.uk